Forewords

I was first introduced to SAQ several years ago and was immediately able to see the huge potential it possessed. Having played and coached both nationally and internationally for many years, to come across such a programme was refreshingly stimulating. When I decided to introduce SAQ to the players in our High Performance Programme, the feedback from everyone was very positive. One player's ranking jumped from number 48 in her region to number 105 world ranking within an 18-month period – a fantastic achievement.

After introducing SAQ into the primary school sector as part of our Junior Tennis Programme, the feedback from both teachers and pupils was again extremely positive. The teachers not only noticed how their pupils improved their tennis skills, but also observed that their self-esteem and confidence grew week by week. They even noticed how it enhanced their general development during their 'skill-hungry' years.

Therefore, from the grass roots to the elite professional, I would strongly urge you to seriously consider using SAQ within your programmes, not only in tennis but in any sports-related environment.

Jerry Lyons
Tennis Director
Alpha Tennis Group
SAQ Trainer/Assessor/Agent

The ability to move with speed, agility and quickness is fundamental to successful tennis performance. These essential movement skills can and should be taught to all players, regardless of age or ability, and in *SAQ Tennis* Alan Pearson has once again developed an invaluable resource for coaches, showing clearly and simply how to design and implement the various stages of the SAQ Continuum into daily tennis practice.

Having benefited from the knowledge and expertise of Alan and the SAQ team for a number of years, I feel sure that anyone wishing to improve their own tennis performance or the performance of those that they coach will achieve tremendous results if they follow the guidance provided by this superb book.

Richie Whall
(MSc, BSc, CSCS, SAQ Advanced Trainer)

v

Introduction

Tennis is one of the most popular and widely played sports in the world and is enjoyed by players of all ages, both male and female. The game places incredible physical demands on those who play it. It is a multi-directional, explosive, stop–start, complex and skilful game. Over the past 30 years not only have players become faster and more powerful, but due to new technologies and materials in tennis racket and ball design the game has also become more power- and speed-based. Average first serve speeds in excess of 125 mph have been recorded at major tournaments, confirming that power and explosive speed dominate, while the interval nature of the modern game is best highlighted by the fact that rallies can last an average of 3–10 seconds (depending on the playing surface), yet matches can take anything from 40 minutes to as long as two hours to complete. The game is incredibly athletic, full of power but also majestic and graceful, and there is nothing more exhilarating than the sight of two elite tennis players competing at a major tournament demonstrating wonderful footwork, pinpoint accuracy and athletic prowess while all the time trying to out-manoeuvre and out-wit their opponent. The control and athletic ability demonstrated when a player is drawn to the net, only for their opponent to lob the ball so they have to turn on the spot, explode using quick feet to get back to the base line and, under extreme pressure, execute a skilful accurate return, is fantastic to watch. Tennis has all the wonderful ingredients of athletic ability, drama, skill and competitiveness that make it not only a great game to play, but also one that is irresistible to watch. These wonderful acts of speed, agility and quickness are what make the difference between winning and losing at whatever level the game is played. In the past, physical attributes such as speed, agility and quickness were thought to be God-given gifts, and were therefore neglected on the training and conditioning field. Today, however, coaches, commentators and players admire these abilities and believe they are essential for success in the game of tennis. More than ever, training and conditioning that include speed, agility and explosive acceleration need to be trained and practised.

The SAQ Tennis Programme is the first ever tennis-specific training and conditioning programme that focuses on the key areas of speed, agility and quickness. The programme also has other significant benefits such as reducing injuries, improving visual awareness skills, improving hand and foot co-ordination and developing strength and core control, as well as being full of variety, challenging and fun for all players. The programme has been developed over many years of work with international and European governing bodies, and players and coaches from around the world. The secret lies in the SAQ Continuum and the use of progressive sequential learning techniques, breaking down complex sports science and making it easy to understand and practical to use. The SAQ Continuum caters for long-term athletic development and multi-skilled training. The end result is the development of multi-directional explosive speed that is specific to the needs of the tennis player. This unique programme can be adapted to meet the needs of all ages, and can be used for both squad training and individual players within a squad. The programme also provides a fantastic opportunity for coaches, trainers and parents to develop new skills and drills, increasing their professionalism.

Contents

Acknowledgements

I would like to thank the International Tennis Federation and Adrian Rattenbury, President of RPT Europe, for providing me with the opportunity to present to and meet many of the top professional coaches throughout Europe at workshops and conferences. A big thank you to all SAQ training directors and administration staff, who provided ongoing encouragement and support while this book was being written. A very special thank you to David Hawkins, Marc Finney, Sarah Naylor, Angus Nicol, Brian Benjamin, Danny Barradale, Amanda Baker and Michael Callow. Also, thank you to all of our SAQ agents and trainers who continue to provide SAQ services throughout the UK and Europe.

The illustrations for this book have been produced by Stephen Gilbert, whose incredible work continues to amaze me. His attention to detail and IT skills have made this book one of the best that SAQ has written so far. Also, a massive thank you and lots of love to Silvana, my wife, who has provided administrative support for the writing of this book.

And finally, a big thank you to Jerry Lyons of the Alpha Tennis Group and two of his star players, John Miller and Lydia Hammond, for helping out at the photoshoot.

Alan Pearson
May 2006

This book enables coaches, trainers, parents and players to understand how and why SAQ Programmes work. It provides clear precise examples of how to put the theory into practice in the training arena. Its progressive structure even covers tennis-specific drills and allows SAQ Training to be integrated into all tennis training sessions.

What is SAQ Training?

Speed has long been considered as just a matter of how fast an object can go from point A to point B. Only recently has speed been studied and broken down into stages such as acceleration, the 'planing out' phase, deceleration and so on. However, much of this research has been carried out by sports coaches involved in straight-line running, so the jumping, turning and zigzagging speed necessary in tennis has been somewhat neglected.

Those involved with the development of SAQ Programmes have sought to fill this void so as to develop all types of speed, particularly for team sports and individual sports such as tennis. SAQ Programmes break speed down into three main areas of skill: speed, agility and quickness. Although these may appear to be similar, they are in fact quite different in terms of how they are trained, developed and integrated into a player's performance. When these skills are successfully combined and specialist SAQ Equipment is utilised, they provide the coach with the tools to make a good player into an outstanding one. It is remarkable what players can achieve with an SAQ Programme.

Speed

A crucial part of any player's game is the ability to cover the ground efficiently and economically over the first few yards and then be able to change direction instantly using explosive footwork, as well as having the ability to open up stride length and increase stride frequency for longer distances. Speed means the maximum velocity a player can achieve and maintain. In most humans the ability to maintain this maximum velocity is for a short period of time and distance only. Speed can also be measured by the amount of time it takes a player to cover a particular distance.

Training to improve maximum speed requires a great deal of focus on correct running mechanics, stride length and frequency, the leg cycle and hip height and position. Drills such as the 'dead-leg run' and stride frequency drills, which are used to help develop an economical running technique, can all be easily integrated into a training session. When working with tennis players, the most effective structure is to focus initially on the development of sound movement mechanics. Once these have been perfected, tennis-specific movement mechanics can be introduced and developed. Tennis-specific mechanics that are not built upon sound fundamental movement mechanics are more likely to fail than to succeed.

The best sprinters spend very little time in contact with the ground and what contact they do make is extremely efficient and powerful. This is no different for tennis players. Focusing on the mechanics of running helps to control and use this power efficiently and sparingly. Training when fresh is also crucial for an athlete/player to attain maximum speed. Many athletes can only reproduce top speeds for a few weeks of the year, but the inclusion and practice of correct running mechanics on the training field will bring great benefit. How often have you seen a tennis player run as if they are also playing a kettledrum, that is with poor arm mechanics? Such a running style will have a detrimental effect on the overall performance and, importantly, the speed of the player with racket in hand or not.

Agility

Agility is the ability to change direction without the loss of dynamic balance, strength, speed or body control. There is a direct link between improved agility and the development of an individual's timing, rhythm and movement.

Agility should not be taken for granted and can actually be taught to individual players. Agility training ensures that a tennis player develops the best all-round court skills possible with the greatest quickness, speed and control and the least amount of wasted energy and movement. Agility also has many other benefits for the individual, helping to prevent niggling injuries and teaching the muscles how to fire properly and control minute shifts in ankle, knee, hip, back, shoulder and neck joints for optimum body alignment. Another very important benefit is that agility training is long lasting. Unlike speed, stamina and weight training, it does not have to be maintained for the individual to retain the benefits. Consider the elderly person who can still ride a bicycle 40 years after having last ridden one. Agility training acts like an indelible mark, programming muscle memory.

THE FOUR ELEMENTS OF AGILITY

There are four elements to agility:

- dynamic balance

- co-ordination

- programmed agility

- random agility.

Within these there is speed, strength, timing and rhythm.

Dynamic balance is a foundation of athleticism and can be taught and retained relatively quickly. Here we teach the ability to stand, stop and walk by focusing on the centre of gravity. Examples include standing on one leg, walking on a balance beam, standing on a balance beam, standing on an agility disc, walking backwards with your eyes closed and jumping on a mini trampoline and then freezing. It does not take too long to train balance. It requires only a couple of minutes, two or three times a week, and should be done early in the morning and early in a training session.

Dynamic balance is complicated by additional stresses. **Co-ordination** involves mastering simple skills under more difficult stresses. Co-ordination work is often slow and methodical with an emphasis on correct biomechanics during athletically demanding movements. Co-ordination can be trained by breaking a skill down into sections then gradually bringing them together. Co-ordination activities include footwork drills, tumbling, rolling and jumping. More difficult examples are walking on a balance beam while playing catch, running along a line while a partner lightly pulls and pushes you in an attempt to move you off the line and jumping onto and off an agility disc while holding a jelly ball.

The third element of agility training is called **programmed agility**. This involves a player who has already experienced the skill or stress that is to be placed on him/her and is aware of the pattern and sequence of demands of that experience. In short, the player has already been programmed. Programmed agility drills can be conducted at high speeds, but must be learned at low, controlled speeds. Examples are zigzag marker drills, shuttle runs, T-marker drills and a lateral shuffle then forward and back, all of which involve changes of direction along a known, standardised pattern. There is no spontaneity. Once these types of drills have been learned and performed on a regular basis, times and performances will improve and advances in strength, explosion, flexibility and body control will be witnessed. This is true of players of any ability.

The final element, and the most difficult to master, prepare for and perform, is **random agility**. Here the player performs tasks with unknown patterns and unknown demands. The coach can incorporate visual and audible reactive skills so that the player has to make split-second decisions with movements based upon the various stimuli. The skill level is now becoming much closer to actual game situations. Random agility can be trained by games such as tag, dodge ball, tennis ball reaction drills and more specific training such as jumping and landing followed by an immediate unexpected movement demand from the coach or training partner.

Agility training is challenging, fun and exciting. There is the opportunity for tremendous variety and training should not become boring or laborious. Agility is not just for those with elite sporting abilities – try navigating through a busy shopping mall!

Quickness

When a player accelerates, a great deal of force has to be generated and transferred through the foot to the ground. This action is similar to that of rolling up a towel (the 'leg'), holding one end in your hand and flicking it out to achieve a cracking noise from the other end (the 'foot'). The act of acceleration takes the body from a static position to motion in a fraction of a second. Muscles actually lengthen and then shorten instantaneously – that is, an 'eccentric' followed by a 'concentric' contraction. This process is known as the stretch shortening cycle action (SSC). SAQ Training concentrates on improving the neuro-muscular system that impacts on this process, so that this initial movement – whether lateral, linear or vertical – is automatic, explosive and precise. The reaction time is the time it takes for the brain to receive and respond to a stimulus by sending a message to the muscle, causing it to

contract. This is what helps a tennis player to cut right, then left, then explode to the net, turn and accelerate back to the base line. With ongoing SAQ Training, the neuro-muscular system is reprogrammed and restrictive mental blocks and thresholds are removed. Consequently, messages from the brain have a clear path to the muscles, and the result is an instinctively quicker player.

Quickness training begins with 'innervation' – isolated fast contractions of an individual joint, for example repeating the same explosive movement over a short period of time, such as fast feet and line drills. These quick repetitive motions take the body through the gears, moving it in a co-ordinated manner to develop speed. Integrating quickness training throughout the year by using fast feet and reaction-type drills will result in the muscles having increased firing rates. This means that players will be capable of faster, more controlled acceleration. The goal is to ensure that your players explode over the first 1–5 yards. Imagine that the firing between the nervous system and the muscles are the gears in a car; the timing, speed and smoothness of the gear change means the wheels and thus the car accelerate away efficiently, with balance and co-ordination, so that the wheels do not spin and the car does not lose control.

Movement skills

Many elements of balance and co-ordination involve the processing of sensory information from within the body. Proprioceptors are sensors that detect muscular tension, tension in tendons, relative tension and pressure in the skin. In addition, the body has a range of other sensors that detect balance. The ability to express balance and co-ordination is highly dependent on the effectiveness of the body's internal sensors and proprioceptors, just like the suspension on a car. Through training, these sensors, and the neural communication system within the body, become more able to interpret these messages and formulate the appropriate movement response. This physiological development underpins effective movement and future movement skill development.

FUNDAMENTAL SKILLS

In today's society many children do not experience appropriate movement opportunities necessary for the development of basic movement abilities (Walkley et al., 1993). It is vital that children experience the full range of the skills listed in the table below (Sugden et al., 1998) if they are going to become competent tennis players in the future.

Fundamental movement skills		
Stability	**Locomotion**	**Manipulation**
Bending	Walking	Throwing
Stretching	Running	Catching
Twisting	Jumping	Kicking
Turning	Hopping	Trapping
Swinging	Skipping	Striking
Inverted supports	Galloping	Volleying
Body rolling	Sliding	Bouncing
Landing/stopping	Leaping	Ball rolling
Dodging	Climbing	Punting

From *Development PE for All Children* by David L Gallahue and F Cleland Donnelly

SAQ Equipment

SAQ Equipment adds variety and stimulus to your training session. Drill variations are unlimited and, once mastered, the results achieved can be quite astonishing. Players of all ages and abilities enjoy the challenges presented to them when training with SAQ Equipment, particularly when introduced in a tennis-specific manner.

When using SAQ Equipment, coaches, trainers and players must be aware of the safety issues involved and of the reduced effectiveness and potentially dangerous consequence of using inappropriate or inferior equipment.

The following pages introduce a variety of SAQ Equipment recommended for use in many of the drills detailed later in this book.

FAST FOOT LADDERS

These are made of webbing, with round, hard plastic rungs spaced approximately 18 inches apart; they come in sets of two pieces each measuring 15 feet. The pieces can be joined together or used as two separate ladders; they can also be folded over to create different angles for players to perform drills on. Fast Foot Ladders are great for improving agility and for the development of explosive fast feet.

MICRO AND MACRO V HURDLES

These come in two sizes: Micro V Hurdles measuring 7 inches and Macro V Hurdles measuring 12 inches in height. They are constructed of a hard plastic and have been specifically designed as a safe freestanding piece of equipment. It is recommended that the hurdles be used in sets of 6–8 to perform the mechanics drills detailed later in the book. They are ideal for practising running mechanics and low-impact plyometrics. The Micro V Hurdles are also great for lateral work.

SONIC CHUTE

These are made from webbing (the belt), nylon cord and a lightweight cloth 'chute', the size of which may vary from 5 to 6 feet. The belt has a release mechanism that, when pulled, drops the chute so that the player can explode forwards. Sonic chutes are great for developing sprint endurance.

VIPER BELT

This is a resistance belt specially made for high-intensity training. It has three stainless steel anchor points where a flexi-cord can be attached. The flexi-cord is made from surgical tubing with a specific elongation. The Viper Belt has a safety belt and safety fasteners; it is double stitched and provides a good level of resistance. This piece of equipment is useful for developing explosive speed in all directions.

SIDE-STEPPERS

These are padded ankle straps that are connected together by an adjustable flexi-cord. They are useful for the development of lateral movements.

REACTOR

This is a rubber ball specifically shaped so that it bounces in unpredictable directions.

OVERSPEED TOW ROPE

This is made up of two belts and a 50-yard nylon cord pulley system. It can be used to provide resistance and is specifically designed for the development of express overspeed and swerve running.

BREAK-AWAY BELT

This is a webbing belt that is connected by Velcro-covered strips. It is good for mirror drills and position-specific marking drills, breaking apart when one player gets away from the other.

STRIDE FREQUENCY CANES

These are plastic, 4-foot long canes of different colours that are used to mark out stride patterns.

SPRINT SLED

This is a metal sled with a central area that can accommodate different weights and a running harness that is attached by webbing straps of 8–20 yards in length.

JELLY BALLS

These are round, soft rubber balls filled with a water-based jelly-like substance. They come in different weights from 4 to 18 lb. They differ from old-fashioned medicine balls in that they can be bounced with great force on to hard surfaces.

HAND WEIGHTS

These are foam-covered weights of 1.5–2.5 lb. They are safe and easy to use both indoors and out.

VISUAL ACUITY RING

This is a hard plastic ring approximately 30 inches in diameter with four different coloured balls attached to it, equally distributed around the ring. The ring helps to develop visual acuity and tracking skills when thrown and caught between players.

PERIPHERAL VISION STICK

This stick is simple but very effective for training peripheral vision. It is approximately 4 feet long with a brightly coloured ball at one end. Once again, it is effective for all players.

BUNT BAT

This is a 4-foot stick with three coloured balls, one at each end and one in the middle. Working in pairs, player 1 holds the bat with two hands while player 2 throws a small ball or beanbag for player 1 to 'bunt' or fend off. This is effective for all players, particularly for hand–eye co-ordination.

AGILITY DISC

This is an inflatable rubber disc 18 inches across. The discs are multi-purpose, but are particularly good for proprioreceptive and core development work (strengthening the deep muscles of the trunk). Players can stand, kneel, sit or lie on the discs to perform all types of drill.

SIDESTRIKE

This is a heavy-duty platform with raised angled ends for foot placement. The ends are adjustable to accommodate different sized athletes and the surface is padded to provide protection. This is a fantastic piece of equipment for explosive footwork development, and is ideal for tennis players.

The SAQ Continuum

Many games activities are characterised by explosive movements, acceleration and deceleration, agility, turning ability and speed of responses (Smythe, 2000). The SAQ Continuum is the sequence and progression of components that make up an SAQ Training session. The progressive elements include tennis-specific patterns of running and drills, including ball work. The Continuum is also flexible and, once the pre-season foundation work has been completed, during the season when time and recovery are of the essence short combination SAQ Training sessions provide a constant top-up to the skills that have already been learned.

SAQ Training is like any other fitness training – if neglected then players' explosive multi-directional power will diminish. The component parts of the SAQ Continuum and how they relate to tennis are:

- **Dynamic Flex** – warm-up on the move

- **Mechanics of movement** – the development of running form for tennis

- **Innervation** – fast feet, agility and control for tennis

- **Accumulation of potential** – the bringing together of the previous components in an SAQ Training tennis circuit

- **Explosion** – the development of explosive three-step multi-directional acceleration for tennis

- **Expression of potential** – short competitive team games that prepare the players for the next level of training

- **Warm-down**.

CHAPTER 1   DYNAMIC FLEX

WARM-UP ON THE MOVE

It is common knowledge and practice that before engaging in intense or strenuous exercise the body should be prepared. The warm-up should achieve a change in a number of physiological responses in order that the body can work safely and effectively:

- increased body temperature, specifically core (deep) muscle temperature
- increased heart rate and blood flow
- increased breathing rate
- increased elasticity of muscular tissues
- activated mental alertness.

The warm-up should take a player from a rested state to the physiological state required for participation in the session that is to follow. The warm-up should gradually increase in intensity as the session goes on. In addition, it should be fun and stimulating for the players, switching them on mentally.

In the past, the standard training session for tennis would begin with the players warming up either by jogging around the tennis court or hitting the ball between themselves, then going through a series of static stretches with a focus on the main muscle groups in the body. However, static stretches are not only irrelevant within the game of tennis but are also more likely to cause injury and loss of power (Kokkonen, Nelson and Cornwell, 1998). Tennis players do not need to be able to do the splits like gymnasts or dancers, but they need to be able to perform dynamic, explosive, multi-directional movements while hitting the ball from all angles around the court. Dynamic Flex is what allows the tennis player to do this: flexibility in action, if you like, combined with power, strength and control.

You do not pull a muscle standing still, so how can you warm it up statically?

Indeed, the most recent research has shown that static stretching before training or competitions can actually be detrimental to performance. Rosenbaum and Hennig (1995) document that static stretching resulted in peak force reduction: a 5 per cent reduction in rate of force production and an 8 per cent decrease in Achilles tendon reflex activity; Oberg (1993) states that static stretching resulted in a decrease in torque during eccentric contractions; Bennett (1999) claims that pre-exercise static stretches decreased eccentric strength by 9 per cent for up to one hour.

The eccentric strength of the muscle is its ability to apply force when lengthening, for instance when a tennis player lands then applies the breaks immediately after a return – his or her ability would typically be reduced by up to 9 per cent for up to an hour after static stretching. Sadly, we still see players performing static stretches not only before the start of the game but also during the game. One of the main arguments in favour of static stretching has been that it helps to prevent injury and muscle soreness. Once again, the latest research suggests the opposite. Gleim and McHugh (1997) state that it is not possible to draw any relationship between flexibility and the risk of injury. Pope (1999) concluded that there was no difference in the occurrence of injury between army recruits who stretched and those who did not. Herbert and Gabriel (2002) suggest that stretching before exercising does not seem to confer a practically useful reduction in the risk of injury. The effects of static stretching on Delayed Onset of Muscle Soreness (DOMS) is inconclusive and the research on this matter is very limited. Smith et al. (1993) report that static stretching led to a higher level of DOMS than a non-stretching group. Herbert and Gabriel (2002) say that 'stretching before or after exercise does not confer protection from muscle soreness'. Getting muscle soreness after physical activity is natural. After a period of time, with continued activity, the body will adapt and cope with the soreness. D.J. McMillian, J.H. Moore, B.S. Hatler and D.C. Taylor (2005) compared the effects of a dynamic warm-up with a static warm-up on power and agility in 30 cadets in the United States Military Academy. Their results strongly confirm that the use of a Dynamic Flex warm-up had a performance enhancement effect and that static stretching did not.

Pre-training and pre-game warm-up

It is important to differentiate between warming up for training and warming up for a game.

PRE-TRAINING WARM-UP

Here Dynamic Flex can be used for 5–20 minutes. The warm-up can be integrated with combination work such as fast feet and mechanics, depending on the time you have allocated. This is also a great time to introduce tennis-specific concepts. Here you can focus on improving a player's ability to perform Dynamic Flex, improving range of movement (ROM) and highlighting positives and negatives of the player's performance. The Dynamic Flex warm-up can be performed using half of the tennis court (see Fig. 1.1). Also included in this chapter are drill variations and the introduction of racket and ball.

PRE-GAME WARM-UP

Here the focus must be on preparing the player to be explosively multi-directional immediately from the first serve. This is not a time to introduce a varied warm-up; keep to a simple, familiar structure so that the player's main focus is the game.

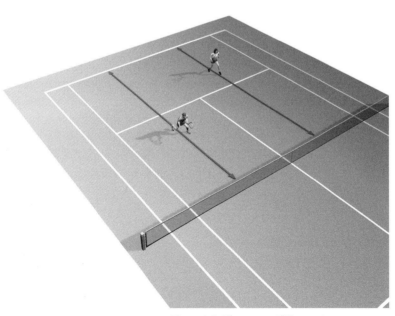

Figure 1.1 Warm-up grid for tennis

The following pre-game structure is recommended:

1 Dynamic Flex   10 minutes

2 Short game practice including   10 minutes
   serves, volley and ground
   strokes

3 Explosive ball drops   3 minutes

4 5 × explosive multi-directional   3 minutes
   acceleration runs –15 yards

There should be no longer than five minutes between the end of the warm-up and the start of the game; any longer and the player will begin to cool down. The pre-game warm-up has been developed so that the player finishes the warm-up explosively and therefore starts the game explosively from the first serve.

Caution

I have recently observed a number of warm-ups comprising a mixture of Dynamic Flex movements and static stretching. The argument by the trainers was that it was the best of both worlds. However, any static stretching – irrespective of the use of dynamic movement patterns – is detrimental to performance prior to training and playing. There should be no static stretching whatsoever at this stage.

DRILL ARM ROLL AND JOG

Aim
To improve shoulder mobility, balance and co-ordination; to increase body temperature; to develop positive foot-to-ground contact.

Area/equipment
Half a tennis court or an indoor or outdoor grid 13 yards in length. Tennis racket and tennis ball.

Description
Player covers the half court or grid by jogging forwards and backwards, rolling the arms forwards so that they move from below the waist to above the head in a rolling motion.

Key teaching points
- The arms should be slightly bent
- Keep off the heels
- Maintain an upright posture
- Ensure there is adequate spacing between players

What you might see	Solutions
■ Arms rotated horizontally	■ Brush the arms past the ears in a more vertical rotational movement
■ Sinking into the hips	■ Breathe in and out lightly, holding the contraction so that normal breathing can occur

Sets and reps
2 × 13 yards (base line to the net), forwards and backwards.

Variations/progressions
- Perform the drill with a racket and ball in hand
- Perform the drill laterally

DRILL SPOTTY DOGS

Aim
To improve shoulder and arm mobility; to activate the core muscles; to improve balance and co-ordination; to increase body temperature.

Area/equipment
Half a tennis court or an indoor or outdoor grid 13 yards in length. Tennis racket and tennis ball.

Description
Player covers the half court or grid by simultaneously 'chopping' the legs and arms, left leg to left arm, right leg to right arm. The range of movement for the arm is from the side of the body up to the side of the face.

Key teaching points
- Keep off the heels
- The arm action is a chop, not a punch
- Land and take off on the balls of the feet
- Maintain an upright posture
- Keep the head up

What you might see
- Players landing flat-footed

- Jerky, unbalanced movements, poor co-ordination

Solutions
- Ensure the player works on the balls of the feet by leaning slightly forwards
- Develop a rhythm by getting the players to call out 'out, in, out, in' while they perform the drill, the calls coinciding with the movement of the legs and arms

Sets and reps
2 × 13 yards (base line to the net), forwards and backwards.

Variation/progression
Players can perform the drill using opposite arms and legs, i.e. right arm to left leg and left arm to right leg.

DRILL   JOG AND HUG

Aim
To improve shoulder and chest mobility; to improve balance and co-ordination; to increase body temperature.

Area/equipment
Half a tennis court or an indoor or outdoor grid 13 yards in length. Tennis racket and tennis ball.

Description
Player covers the half court or grid by slowly jogging forwards, bringing the arms around the front of the body so the fingers can grip behind the opposite shoulder. Alternate the arms over and under.

Key teaching points
- Squeeze slowly
- Ensure there is adequate spacing between players
- Jog on the balls of the feet
- Maintain an upright posture

What you might see	Solutions
Trunk held too upright	Player should tilt the trunk slightly forwards and drop the chin closer to the chest
Running on the heels	Lean the body forwards – this will push the weight onto the balls of the feet

Sets and reps
2 × 13 yards (base line to the net), forwards and backwards.

Variation/progression
Squeeze and then rotate the core, turning from left to right, right to left.

DRILL   STAR JUMPS

Aim
To improve shoulder mobility; to improve balance and co-ordination; to develop positive foot-to-ground contact.

Area/equipment
Half a tennis court or an indoor or outdoor grid 13 yards in length. Tennis racket and tennis ball.

Description
Players work on the spot, bringing their arms out and above the head so that the inside of the arms are nearly touching the ears and the hands come together above the head, while simultaneously the legs are split out in a jumping movement. The legs are then brought together at the same time as the arms are brought back to the sides.

Key teaching points
- Develop a rhythm
- Do not sink into the hips
- Stay tall
- Land and take off on the balls of the feet, not on the heels
- Ensure there is adequate spacing between players

What you might see
- Sinking into the hips on landing

- Deep bending of the knees on landing

Solutions
- Player can breathe in, breathe out, breathe in again and hold the contraction in order to breathe comfortably while performing the drill
- Player should land on the balls of the feet with firm knees, with only a slight give

Sets and reps
20 star jumps.

Variation/progression
Alternate the basic drill with bringing the arms out above the front of the head, then alternate with bringing the arms above the side of the head.

DRILL WALKING ON THE BALLS OF THE FEET

Aim
To stretch the shins and improve ankle mobility; to improve balance and co-ordination; to increase body temperature.

Area/equipment
Half a tennis court or an indoor or outdoor grid 13 yards in length. Tennis racket and tennis ball.

Description
Player covers the half court or grid by walking on the balls of the feet, then returns to the start by repeating the drill backwards while handling the ball.

Key teaching points
- Do not walk on the toes
- Keep off the heels
- Maintain correct arm mechanics
- Maintain an upright posture
- Squeeze buttocks together

What you might see	Solutions
Walking on the toes	Player should focus on walking on the balls of the feet, keeping the head horizontal with the body leaning slightly forwards
Legs too wide apart	Feet should be shoulder-width apart – use marker dots for spacing if necessary

Sets and reps
2 × 13 yards (base line to the net), forwards and backwards.

Variation/progression
Perform the drill with the arms stretched out above the head. This will challenge balance and core control.

DRILL LATERAL WALKING ON THE BALLS OF THE FEET

Aim
To stretch the shins and improve ankle mobility; to improve lateral balance and co-ordination; to increase body temperature.

Area/equipment
Half a tennis court or an indoor or outdoor grid 13 yards in length. Tennis racket and tennis ball.

Description
Player covers the half court or grid by walking sideways on the balls of the feet, then returns to the start by repeating the drill in the opposite sideways direction.

Key teaching points
- Do not bring the feet completely together
- Do not cross the feet
- Do not walk on the toes
- Keep off the heels
- Maintain correct arm mechanics
- Maintain an upright posture
- Keep the hips square
- Feet should be shoulder-width apart
- Keep the head up

What you might see	Solutions
Crossing of feet	Keep the hips square
Loss of balance	Drop the heels to just above the ground
Strides too long	Ensure the feet are shoulder-width apart
Bringing the feet together	Ensure the feet are shoulder-width apart

Sets and reps
2 × 13 yards (base line to the net), 1 with the left shoulder leading and 1 with the right shoulder leading.

Variation/progression
Hold the arms above the head.

DRILL ANKLE FLICKS

Aim
To stretch the calves and improve ankle mobility; to improve balance, co-ordination and rhythm of movement; to prepare for good foot-to-floor contact; to increase body temperature.

Area/equipment
Half a tennis court or an indoor or outdoor grid 13 yards in length. Tennis racket and tennis ball.

Description
Player covers the half court or grid in a skipping motion where the balls of the feet plant then flick up towards the shin. The player should move in a rhythmic, bouncing manner. The player then returns to the start by repeating the drill backwards.

Key teaching points
- Work off the balls of the feet, not the toes
- Practise the first few steps on the spot before moving off
- Maintain correct arm mechanics
- Maintain an upright posture

What you might see	Solutions
Poor plantar/dorsiflex range of movement (raising and lowering of the toes)	Player can pull toes towards the shin on the upward flick
Jerky, un-rhythmic movement	Player can call 'up, down' or 'one, two' to help with rhythm

Sets and reps
2×13 yards (base line to the net), forwards and backwards.

Variation/progression
Perform the drill laterally.

DRILL   *SMALL SKIP*

Aim
To improve lower leg flexibility and ankle mobility; to improve balance, co-ordination and rhythm; to develop positive foot-to-ground contact; to increase body temperature.

Area/equipment
Half a tennis court or an indoor or outdoor grid 13 yards in length. Tennis racket and tennis ball.

Description
Player covers the half court or grid in a low skipping motion, then returns to the start by repeating the drill backwards.

Key teaching points
- Raise knee to an angle of about 45–55 degrees
- Work off the balls of the feet
- Maintain correct arm mechanics
- Maintain an upright posture
- Maintain a good rhythm

What you might see   Solutions
- Too high knee lift
- Poor rhythm

- Player to focus on the knee not coming any higher than the waistband
- Same as above

Sets and reps
2 × 13 yards (base line to the net), forwards and backwards.

Variation/progression
Perform the drill laterally.

DRILL · WIDE SKIP

Aim
To improve hip and ankle mobility; to improve balance, co-ordination and rhythm; to increase body temperature.

Area/equipment
Half a tennis court or an indoor or outdoor grid 13 yards in length. Tennis racket and tennis ball.

Description
Player covers the half court or grid by skipping. The feet should remain wider than shoulder-width apart and the knees should face outwards at all times. The player then returns to the start by repeating the drill backwards. The drill should be performed with a ball in the hand.

Key teaching points
- Keep off the heels
- Maintain correct arm mechanics
- Maintain an upright posture
- Do not take the thigh above a 90-degree angle

What you might see	Solutions
Landing on flat feet	Players should lean slightly forwards – ask them to focus their eyes on an object 15–20 yards ahead on the floor
Arms and elbows held in too tight to the body	Encourage good arm drive – the inside of the wrist should brush the hips and the thumb should come up to the side of the face

Sets and reps
2 × 13 yards (base line to the net), forwards and backwards.

Variation/progression
Perform the drill laterally.

DRILL   KNEE-OUT SKIP

Aim
To stretch the inner thigh and improve hip mobility; to develop an angled knee drive, balance, co-ordination and rhythm; to increase body temperature.

Area/equipment
Half a tennis court or an indoor or outdoor grid 13 yards in length. Tennis racket and tennis ball.

Description
Player covers the half court or grid in a skipping motion. The knee moves from the centre of the body to a position outside the body before returning to the central position. The player then returns to the start by repeating the drill backwards. The ball is held out at an angle to provide a target for the knee.

Key teaching points
- The feet start in a linear position and move outwards as the knee is raised
- Work off the balls of the feet
- The knee is to be pushed, not rolled, out and back
- Maintain correct arm mechanics
- The movement should be smooth, not jerky

What you might see
- Landing on the heels

- Leaning too far back

Solutions
- Focus on landing on the balls of the feet, with the trunk leaning forwards
- Keep the head slightly dipped towards the chest

Sets and reps
2 × 13 yards (base line to the net), forwards and backwards.

Variation/progression
Perform the drill laterally.

DRILL SINGLE-KNEE DEAD-LEG LIFT

Aim
To improve buttock flexibility and hip mobility; to isolate the correct 'running cycle' motion for each leg.

Area/equipment
Half a tennis court or an indoor or outdoor grid 13 yards in length. Tennis racket and tennis ball.

Description
Player covers the half court or grid by bringing the knee of one leg quickly up to a 90-degree angle. The other leg should remain as straight as possible with a very short lift away from the ground throughout the movement. The ratio should 1:4, i.e. one lift to every four steps. Work one leg on the way down the grid and the other on the return.

Key teaching points
- Do not raise the knees above a 90-degree angle
- Strike the floor with the ball of the foot
- Keep the foot in a linear position
- Maintain correct running mechanics

What you might see / Solutions

What you might see	Solutions
Both knees being lifted	Player should focus on one side only and perform the drill at a walking pace, i.e. walk, lift, walk, lift
Stuttering form and rhythm	Use marker dots to help rhythm and work on this drill in the mechanics phase
Knee lift angled either out or across the body	Player should perform the drill with the arm on the knee-lift side held out in front of them, holding the ball; the knee should be brought up to touch the ball

Sets and reps
2 × 13 yards (base line to the net), forwards and backwards.

Variation/progression
Vary the lift ratio, e.g. 1:2 (one lift to every two steps).

DRILL   HIGH KNEE-LIFT SKIP

Aim
To improve buttock flexibility and hip mobility; to increase range of motion (ROM) over a period of time; to develop rhythm; to increase body temperature.

Area/equipment
Half a tennis court or an indoor or outdoor grid 13 yards in length. Tennis racket and tennis ball.

Description
Player covers the half court or grid in a high skipping motion, then returns to the start by repeating the drill backwards.

Key teaching points
- The thigh should be taken past 90 degrees
- Work off the balls of the feet
- Maintain a strong core
- Maintain an upright posture
- Control the head by looking forwards at all times
- Maintain correct arm mechanics

What you might see
- Landing on the heels

- Inconsistency of knee lift (i.e. to different heights)

Solutions
- Player should lean forwards and focus on the balls of the feet
- The knee should be raised to just above waist. Player should perform the drill at walking pace so the range of movement can be practised

Sets and reps
2 × 13 yards (base line to the net), forwards and backwards.

Variation/progression
Perform the drill laterally.

DRILL KNEE-ACROSS SKIP

Aim
To improve outer hip flexibility and hip mobility over a period of time; to develop balance and co-ordination; to increase body temperature.

Area/Equipment
Half a tennis court or an indoor or outdoor grid 13 yards in length. Tennis racket and tennis ball.

Description
Player covers the half court or grid in a skipping motion where the knee comes across the body, then returns to the start by repeating the drill backwards. The ball is held at an angle away from the body on the same side as the knee performing the skip, to act as a target for the knee.

Key teaching points
■ Do not force an increased ROM
■ Work off the balls of the feet
■ Maintain a strong core
■ Maintain an upright posture
■ Control the head by looking forwards at all times
■ Use the arms primarily for balance

What you might see	Solutions
■ Too high knee lift	■ The ball should be held below waist level
■ Skipping on the heels	■ Player should lean slightly forwards and transfer weight to the balls of the feet

Sets and reps
2 × 13 yards (base line to the net), forwards and backwards.

Variation/progression
Perform the drill laterally.

DRILL   *LATERAL RUNNING*

Aim
To develop an economic knee drive; to stretch the side of the quadriceps; to prepare for an efficient lateral running technique; to increase body temperature.

Area/equipment
Half a tennis court or an indoor or outdoor grid 13 yards in length. Tennis racket and tennis ball.

Description
Player covers the half court or grid with the left or right shoulder leading, taking short lateral steps, then returns with the opposite shoulder leading.

Key teaching points
- Keep the hips square
- Work off the balls of the feet
- Do not skip
- Do not let the feet cross over
- Maintain an upright posture
- Do not sink in to the hips or fold at the waist
- Do not over-stride – use short, sharp steps
- Maintain correct arm mechanics

What you might see	Solutions
Feet crossing or being brought together	Get players to focus on working with their feet shoulder-width apart. The ROM of the feet should be from just outside the shoulder to just inside the shoulder, using the outside of the foot as the gauge
Skipping sideways	Players should focus on a stepping rather than a skipping motion; use marker spots to indicate where the feet should be placed in lateral stepping
No arm movement or arms by the sides	Players should hold a tennis ball in each hand to practise correct arm drive techniques – they should brush the side of their body with the ball and bring the ball up to the side of the face. This will help arm drive

Sets and reps
2 × 13 yards (base line to the net), one leading with the left shoulder and one leading with the right shoulder.

Variation/progression
Practise lateral-angled zigzag runs.

DRILL   *PRE-TURN*

Aim
To prepare the hips for a turning action without committing the whole body; to increase body temperature and improve body control.

Area/equipment
Half a tennis court or an indoor or outdoor grid 13 yards in length. Tennis racket and tennis ball.

Description
Player covers the half court or grid by performing a lateral movement. The heel of the back foot is moved to a position almost alongside the lead foot. Just before the feet come together, the lead foot is moved away laterally. Return to the start by repeating the drill, but lead with the opposite shoulder.

Key teaching points
- The back foot must not cross the lead foot
- Work off the balls of the feet
- Maintain correct arm mechanics
- Maintain an upright posture
- Do not sink into the hips or fold at the waist
- Do not use a high knee-lift; the angle should be no more than 45 degrees

What you might see	Solutions
■ Crossing of feet	■ Players to focus on a stepping rather than a skipping motion; use marker spots to indicate where feet should be placed in pre-turn stepping
■ Leading leg raised	■ Use the arm on the leading side to press down on the thigh as a reminder that this leg remains straighter
■ Hips turned	■ Stand tall with the head up, breathe in and out then hold the contraction

Sets and reps
2 × 13 yards (base line to the net), one leading with the left shoulder and one leading with the right shoulder.

DRILL CARIOCA

Aim
To improve hip mobility and speed, which will increase the firing of nerve impulses over a period of time; to develop balance and co-ordination while moving and twisting; to increase body temperature.

Area/equipment
Half a tennis court or an indoor or outdoor grid 13 yards in length. Tennis racket and tennis ball.

Description
Player covers the half court or grid by moving laterally. The rear foot crosses in front of the body and then moves around to the back. Simultaneously, the lead foot does the opposite. The arms also move across the front and back of the body.

Key teaching points
- Start slowly and gradually build up the tempo
- Work off the balls of the feet
- Keep the shoulders square
- Do not force the ROM
- Use the arms primarily for balance

What you might see

What you might see	Solutions
Sinking into the hips	Stand tall with the head up, breathe in and out and hold the contraction
Co-ordination problems, e.g. unable to put second leg behind front leg	Practise slowly; go through the drill at walking pace
Arms swung too quickly or not at all	Allow the arms to do what comes naturally. The use of the ball may prove difficult at first, so initially practise without the ball

Sets and reps
2 × 13 yards (base line to the net), one leading with the left leg and one leading with the right leg.

Variation/progression
Perform the drill laterally with a partner (mirror drills), i.e. one initiates/leads the movement while the other attempts to follow.

DRILL SIDE LUNGE

Aim
To stretch the inner thighs and gluteals (buttocks); to develop balance and co-ordination; to increase body temperature.

Area/equipment
Half a tennis court or an indoor or outdoor grid 13 yards in length. Tennis racket and tennis ball.

Description
Player covers the half court or grid by performing lateral lunges: take a wide lateral step and simultaneously lower the gluteals towards the ground. Return to the start with the opposite shoulder leading.

Key teaching points
- Do not bend at the waist or lean forwards
- Try to keep off the heels
- Maintain a strong core and keep upright
- Use the arms primarily for balance

What you might see
- Players leaning forwards

Solutions
- Keep the spine in an upright, aligned position by keeping the head up and the chin level

Sets and reps
2 × 13 yards (base line to the net), one leading with the left shoulder and one leading with the right shoulder.

Variation/progression
Work in pairs facing each other and chest-passing the ball.

DRILL HAMSTRING BUTTOCK FLICKS

Aim
To stretch the front and back of the thighs; to improve hip mobility; to increase body temperature.

Area/equipment
Half a tennis court or an indoor or outdoor grid 13 yards in length. Tennis racket and tennis ball.

Description
Player covers the half court or grid by moving forwards using alternating leg flicks, where the heel moves up towards the buttocks, then returns to the start by repeating the drill backwards.

Key teaching points
- Start slowly and gradually build up the tempo
- Work off the balls of the feet
- Maintain an upright posture
- Do not sink into the hips
- Try to develop a rhythm

What you might see	Solutions
Knee raised up towards the front of the body	The thigh should remain vertical to the ground with the movement starting from below the knee. Practise the leg flick while standing still, using a wall or a partner for stability, and get the players to look down and observe the movement required
Hands held at the back above the top of the thighs	Use of the ball should help prevent this negative action; remind players that they do not move with their hands behind their backs during a game

Sets and reps
2 × 13 yards (base line to the net), forwards and backwards.

Variations/progressions
- Perform the drill laterally
- Perform the drill as above, but flick the heel to the outside of the buttocks

To stretch the hamstrings, groin and gluteals; to improve balance and co-ordination; to increase body temperature.

Area/equipment
Half a tennis court or an indoor or outdoor grid 13 yards in length. Tennis racket and tennis ball.

Description
Player covers the half court or grid in a skipping motion where the heel of one leg comes up to almost touch the inside thigh of the opposite leg. Imagine there is a football on a piece of string hanging centrally just below your waist and you are trying to kick it with alternate heels. Return to the start by repeating the drill backwards.

Key teaching points
- Start slowly and gradually build up the tempo
- Work off the balls of the feet
- Maintain an upright posture
- Maintain a strong core throughout
- Use the arms for balance

What you might see	Solutions
Confusion between the high-knee skip and heel to inside of thigh skip	The heel of the lifted leg should be directed towards the inside of the groin. The heel can touch the inside of the thigh as a cue for correct range of movement

Sets and reps
2 × 13 yards (base line to the net), forwards and backwards.

Variation/progression
Perform the drill laterally.

DRILL   SIDEWAYS HEEL FLICKS

Aim
To stretch the gluteals, outer hamstrings and outer thighs; to develop rhythm and co-ordination; to increase body temperature.

Area/equipment
Half a tennis court or an indoor or outdoor grid 13 yards in length. Tennis racket and tennis ball.

Description
Player covers the half court or grid by performing a skipping motion where the heel is flicked up and out to the side, then returns to the start by repeating the drill backwards.

Key teaching points
- Start slowly and gradually build up the tempo
- Work off the balls of the feet
- Maintain an upright posture and a strong core
- Use the arms for balance
- Try to develop a rhythm

What you might see
- Landing on flat feet and too upright

Solutions
- Players should lean slightly forwards and transfer their weight onto the balls of the feet

Sets and reps
2 × 13 yards (base line to the net), forwards and backwards.

Variation/progression
Alternate quickly between left shoulder leading and right shoulder leading while performing the drill.

DRILL HURDLE WALK

Aim
To stretch the inner and outer thighs and increase ROM; to develop balance and co-ordination; to increase body temperature.

Area/equipment
Half a tennis court or an indoor or outdoor grid 13 yards in length. Tennis racket and tennis ball.

Description
Player covers the half court or grid by walking in a straight line and lifting alternate legs as if going over high hurdles, then returns to the start by repeating the drill backwards.

Key teaching points
- Try to keep the body square as the hips rotate
- Work off the balls of the feet
- Maintain an upright posture
- Do not sink into the hips or bend over at the waist
- Imagine that you are actually stepping over a barrier

What you might see
- The anchored foot is flat while the other leg is raised, causing a poor range of movement

Solutions
- Players should focus on working off the ball of the foot that is anchored. Practise this by getting the players to stand with their feet shoulder-width apart, rise up off their heels onto the balls of the feet, hold for a second and then return to the starting position; repeat 20–30 times. This will provide kinaesthetic feedback to the players about what it feels like to be on the balls of the feet

Sets and reps
2 × 13 yards (base line to the net), forwards and backwards.

DRILL   RUSSIAN WALK

Aim
To stretch the back of the thighs; to improve hip mobility and stabilise the ankle; to develop balance and co-ordination; to increase body temperature.

Area/equipment
Half a tennis court or an indoor or outdoor grid 13 yards in length. Tennis racket and tennis ball.

Description
Player covers the half court or grid by performing a walking march with a high extended step. Imagine that the aim is to scrape the sole/spikes of your tennis shoe down the front of a door or a fence.

Key teaching points
- Lift the knee before extending the leg
- Work off the balls of the feet
- Try to keep off the heels, particularly on the back foot
- Keep the hips square
- Pull the toes of the extended leg towards the shin so that they are vertical.

What you might see	Solutions
■ Toes pointing out horizontally, not vertically	■ Get the player to pull the toes towards the shin, and practise the Russian Walk on the spot before trying it on the move

Sets and reps
2 × 13 yards (base line to the net), both forwards.

Variation/progression
Perform the drill backwards.

DRILL WALKING LUNGE

Aim
To stretch the front of the hips and thighs; to develop balance and co-ordination; to increase body temperature.

Area/equipment
Half a tennis court or an indoor or outdoor grid 13 yards in length. Tennis racket and tennis ball.

Description
Player covers the half court or grid by performing a walking lunge. The front leg should be bent with a 90-degree angle at the knee and the thigh in a horizontal position. The back leg should also be bent at a 90-degree angle, but with the knee touching the ground and the thigh in a vertical position. During the lunge the player brings both arms above the head to activate the core muscles. Return to the start by repeating the drill backwards.

Key teaching points
- Keep the hips square
- Maintain a strong core and keep upright
- Maintain good control
- Persevere with backward lunges – they are difficult to master
- Keep the trunk in an upright position

What you might see	Solutions
Poor balance and control	Over-striding can cause this. Ensure that players bend the knee at a 90-degree angle and that the thigh is in the horizontal position. Use marker dots to indicate the length of the lunge
Stride too short, causing inability to lunge properly	Focus on a 90-degree knee bend and ensure that the thigh is horizontal. Practise the drill slowly on the spot if poor form continues

Sets and reps
2 × 13 yards (base line to the net), forwards and backwards.

Variations/progressions
- Perform the drill while holding handweights
- Perform the drill while catching and passing a ball in the down position
- Alternate arms above the head, one up and one down

DRILL | WALKING HAMSTRING

Aim
To stretch the backs of the thighs.

Area/equipment
Half a tennis court or an indoor or outdoor grid 13 yards in length. Tennis racket and tennis ball.

Description
Player covers the half court or grid by extending the lead leg heel first on the ground, rolling onto the ball of the foot and sinking into the hips, keeping the spine upright. Walk forwards and repeat on the opposite leg and continue in this manner, alternating the lead leg. For comfort, cross the arms.

Key teaching points
- Keep the spine straight
- Do not bend over
- Control the head by looking forwards at all times
- Work at a steady pace; do not rush

What you might see
- Players with their head down, leaning forwards
- Bending at the waist

Solutions
- Players should keep the chin up and focus on something horizontally in line with the eyes
- Hips should be kept square; the trunk and spine must remain upright

Sets and reps
2 × 13 yards (base line to the net), forwards and backwards.

Variation/progression
Perform the drill laterally.

DRILL WALL DRILL – LEG OUT AND ACROSS BODY

Aim
To increase the ROM in the hip region; to increase body temperature.

Area/equipment
A wall or fence to lean against.

Description
Player faces and leans against the wall/fence at a 20–30-degree angle and swings the leg across the body from one side to the other. Repeat on the other leg.

Key teaching points
- Do not force an increased ROM
- Work off the ball of the support foot
- Lean with both hands against the wall/fence
- Keep the hips square
- Do not look down
- Gradually speed up the movement

What you might see
- No heel raise off the ground

Solutions
- Get players to focus on leaning forwards and transferring their weight onto the ball of the foot while the other leg is swung across the body. Place the handle of a tennis racket under the heel of the planted foot

Sets and reps
7–10 on each leg.

Variation/progression
Lean against a partner.

DRILL   WALL DRILL – LINEAR LEG FORWARDS/BACK

Aim
To increase the ROM in the hip region; to increase body temperature.

Area/equipment
A wall or fence to lean against.

Description
Player faces and leans against the wall/fence at a 20–30-degree angle, takes the leg back and swings it forwards in a linear motion along the same plane. Repeat with the other leg.

Key teaching points
- Do not force an increased ROM
- Work off the ball of the support foot
- Lean with both hands against the wall/fence
- Do not look down
- Gradually increase the speed of the movement

What you might see
- No heel raise off the ground

Solutions
- Get players to focus on leaning forwards and transferring their weight onto the ball of the foot while the other leg is swung across the body. Place the handle of a tennis racket under the heel of the planted foot

Sets and reps
7–10 on each leg.

Variation/progression
Lean against a partner.

DRILL   WALL DRILL – KNEE ACROSS BODY

Aim
To increase the ROM in the hip region; to increase body temperature.

Area/equipment
A wall or fence to lean against.

Description
The player faces and leans against the wall/fence at a 20–30-degree angle and, from a standing position, drives one knee upwards and across the body. Repeat with the other leg.

Key teaching points
- Do not force an increased ROM
- Work off the ball of the support foot
- Lean with both hands against the wall/fence
- Keep the hips square
- Do not look down
- Gradually increase the speed of the movement
- Imagine you are trying to get your knee up and across your body to the opposite hip

What you mght see
- No heel raise off the ground

Solutions
- Get players to focus on leaning forwards and transferring their weight onto the ball of the foot while the other leg is swung across the body. Place the handle of a tennis racket under the heel of the planted foot

Sets and reps
7–10 on each leg.

Variation/progression
Lean against a partner.

DRILL   *SELECTION OF SPRINTS*

Aim
To increase the intensity of the warm-up and prepare players for maximum exertion; to speed up the firing rate of neuro-muscular messages; to increase body temperature.

Area/equipment
Half a tennis court or an indoor or outdoor grid 13 yards in length. Tennis racket and tennis ball.

Description
Players to sprint one way only, then perform a jog-back recovery back down the grid. Players should start from different angles, e.g. side-on, backwards, etc., and accelerate into a forward running motion down the grid.

Key teaching points
- Maintain good running mechanics
- Ensure that players alternate the lead foot

Sets and reps
1 set of 5 sprints, varying the start position.

Variations/progressions
- Include swerving sprints
- Include turns in the sprints
- Introduce left and right lunges at the end of the sprint
- Introduce a serve at the start of the sprint

DRILL GRID VARIATIONS – ZIGZAG GRID

Aim
To stimulate and motivate players with a variety of movement patterns.

Area/equipment
Mark out the tennis court by placing 8 marker dots or cones as follows: the first on the base line 1 yard away from the side line, the second just before the net or centre line 1 yard away from the side line, and the next six marker dots or cones two yards apart at angles using the single and double side lines as a guide for the width. See Fig. 1.2.

Description
Players should perform Dynamic Flex drills down the grid from the marker on the base line, splitting around the end to return on the outside of the grid. On reaching the side markers, players should zigzag back through them, then return to the starter marker on the base line and repeat, performing a different Dynamic Flex drill.

Key teaching points
Timing is crucial – players should be constantly on the move.

Sets and reps
Players can perform the entire Dynamic Flex warm-up in this manner.

Variation/progression
Replace the markers on the outside of the grid with Fast Foot Ladders or hurdles.

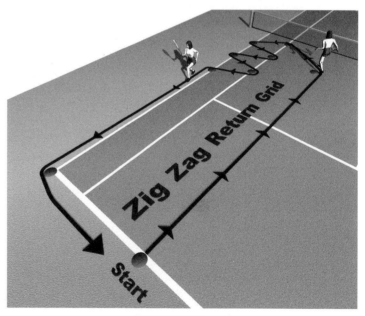

Figure 1.2 Zigzag grid

DRILL GRID VARIATIONS – CIRCLE GRID

Aim
To stimulate and motivate players; to improve and challenge Dynamic Flex movements while moving around a circle.

Area/equipment
Mark out a circular grid with markers within one half of the tennis court, and a centre circle of markers 2 yards in diameter. See Fig. 1.3.

Description
Perform Dynamic Flex around the outside of the circle, changing direction forwards and backwards. Then, for certain drills such as the Hamstring Walk, get the players to move inwards and outwards to and from the centre circle.

Key teaching point
Timing and change of direction are very important.

Sets and reps
Players can perform the entire Dynamic Flex warm-up in this manner.

Variation/progression
Players can warm up while holding a racket.

Figure 1.3 Circle grid

CHAPTER 2 RUNNING FORM FOR TENNIS

THE MECHANICS OF MOVEMENT

Tennis involves a great deal of multi-directional movement, including running. Many years ago, future tennis players would develop a lot of their skills through playing in the streets, on school playing fields and in PE lessons. Incredibly, however, over the past 25–30 years more than 70 per cent of children have not gone on to participate in any sport on leaving school. In some primary schools, children are lucky to get 12 hours of physical activity a year. In addition, governing bodies continue to sell off playgrounds and playing fields for housing developments, with the result that children and teenagers have nowhere to practise. Therefore, one of the most damaging assumptions made by coaches is that players will have been taught to run and move correctly within the education system, or that it is something that occurs naturally. You will always encounter naturally gifted players who are explosive and who make fast running, jumping and side-stepping look easy, but they are few and far between. To neglect running and movement mechanics in your tennis training is to ignore the potential in many of your players.

One often hears comments in the game of tennis such as 'if I'd only moved more quickly I would have been able to reach the ball!' or 'good technical skills but too slow'. Many young players lack the dynamic balance, co-ordination, visual awareness and general running and movement skills to be able to react to the speed of the game. All players, whatever their age, can improve their speed, acceleration and general movement skills by practising and applying the correct mechanics.

The best players in the world are able to control the pace of their play effectively and economically. They have the ability to turn up the intensity on the opposition by being quicker around the court, being faster and more accurate in their positioning and generally reacting more explosively than the opposition.

The game of tennis can be best described as a multi-directional, explosive, stop–start activity with players maintaining dynamic balance and control so they can effectively hit the ball. In an average point there are four changes of direction (Roetert and Ellenbecker, 1998). Recent analysis conducted at a Grand Slam tournament to obtain a better understanding of the types of movement patterns used in tennis confirmed that the distances covered while playing strokes are short and explosive (see Fig. 2.1): 80 per cent of all strokes are played within less than 2.5 metres of movement with the player in a standing position; approximately 10 per cent of all strokes are made within 2.5–4.5 metres of movement with a sliding/shuffle movement pattern; and fewer than 5 per cent of strokes are made with greater than 4.5 metres of movement using a running type pattern of movement (Ferrauti and Weber, 2001).

There are two types of mechanics for tennis. The first is foundation mechanics, which focuses on the development of fundamental movement patterns. The second is tennis-specific mechanics, which focuses on the development of tennis-specific movement patterns. Fundamental movement mechanics are crucial: if a player can't run and move properly without a racket, he/she will find it even more difficult to run and move properly when holding a racket.

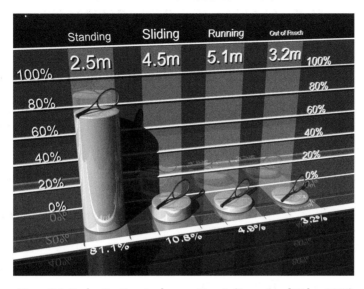

Figure 2.1 Stroke situations in clay-court tennis (Ferrauti and Weber, 2001)

Foundation mechanics

ARM MECHANICS

There is no need to focus on techniques for the 100 m sprint – tennis players very rarely have the space to 'plane out' after 30 m or relax and think about 'jelly jaw' exercises. Tennis requires a sound basic technique: the ability to change from correct running mechanics to bending and half-volleying the ball off the ground, decelerating while returning to a more upright body position and at the same time reasserting good mechanics to change direction and re-accelerate to the other side of the court.

Remember that many coaches and managers are first and foremost looking for the players who are explosive over the first five yards. Using the correct arm drive will go a long way to assisting players of all shapes and sizes to be quicker in this area.

Running form – arms
- Elbows should be held at 90 degrees
- Hands and shoulders should be relaxed
- The insides of the wrists should brush against the pockets
- The hands should move from the buttock cheeks to the chest or head

LIFT MECHANICS

Coaching players to get their knees up high, particularly in the first few yards of the acceleration phase, only makes them slower. Using a high knee lift during the acceleration phase has the negative effect of minimising force development, resulting in not enough power being produced to propel the body forwards in an explosive action. During the first few yards of acceleration, short, sharp steps are required. These steps generate a high degree of force, which takes the body from a stationary position into the first controlled explosive steps.

Tennis is a multi-sprint stop-and-start sport, so the first phase of acceleration and re-acceleration are crucial. Look and listen for the following in a player's initial acceleration strides:

- 45-degree knee lift

- Foot-to-floor contact with the balls of the feet

- Front of the foot staying in a linear position

- Knees coming up in a vertical line

- Foot-to-floor contact making a tapping noise, not a thud or a slap

- The foot and knee should not splay in or out, or power will not be transferred correctly

- Keeping off the heels

- On the lift, the foot will transfer from pointing slightly down to pointing slightly up

POSTURE

Posture is a crucial part of all movements required for tennis, including sprinting, jumping and turning. The spine should be kept as straight as possible at all times. This means that a player who has jumped for the ball and now has to run into space needs to transfer to the correct running form as quickly as possible. Running with a straight spine does not mean running bolt upright – you can keep your spine straight using a slight forward lean. What *is* to be avoided is players running while sinking into their hips, which makes them look like they are being folded up in the middle, or sinking too deep when landing after jumping, which prevents an instant and effective transfer of power.

Core control is another important factor in developing and utilising strong posture. Core development and maintenance for tennis players is very important and will be touched on briefly later in this book. A simple rule prior to and throughout the performing of all the drills in this book is as follows: engage your core muscles by simply breathing in, breathing out and breathing in again; then try to maintain this feeling throughout the exercise, not forgetting to breathe normally! This will help prevent the pelvic wall from moving around, which causes a loss of power, and will also protect the lower back, hamstrings and girdle area from injury.

MECHANICS FOR DECELERATION

The ability of a tennis player to stop quickly, change direction and accelerate away after hitting the ball is crucial for success. You can practise this – do not leave it to chance.

- **Posture**: lean back. This alters the angle of the spine and hips, which control foot placement. Foot contact with the ground will now transfer to the heels, which act like a brake.

- **Fire the arms**: by firing the arms quickly, the energy produced will increase the frequency of heel contact to the ground. Think of it like pressing harder on the brakes in a car.

The running techniques described in this chapter cover basic mechanics for tennis-specific techniques where running, jumping and turning are all important parts of the game. The techniques are developed through the use of hurdles, stride frequency canes and running technique drills.

LATERAL SIDE-STEP

Do not use a wide stance as this will decrease the potential for power generation as you attempt to push off/away. Do not pull with the leading foot, but rather push off the back foot. Imagine that your car has broken down and that you need to move it to a service station – would you pull it? No, you would push it. Ensure that a strong arm drive is used at all times, but particularly during the push-off phase.

MAKING A 180-DEGREE TURN – THE DROP STEP

Most players use too many movements to make a 180-degree turn. Many jump up on the spot first, then take three or four steps to make the turn; others will jump up and perform the turn in the air with a complete lack of control. When practised, the drop step turn looks seamless and is far quicker.

For a right shoulder turn, the player starts by opening up the right groin and simultaneously transferring the weight onto the left foot. The right foot is raised slightly off the ground and, using a swinging action, is moved around to the right to face the opposite direction. The right foot is planted and the player drives/pushes off the left foot, remembering to use a strong arm drive. Do not overstretch on the turn. Players may find it helpful initially to tell themselves to 'turn and go'. With practice, players will develop an efficient and economic seamless turn.

Fundamental movement checklists for players

The movement checklists for players will help coaches and trainers identify correct and incorrect form for multi-directional movement. They also provide solutions that can be simply implemented to rectify the problems. These solutions can be used with players of all ages and abilities. If you are ever in doubt regarding a player's movement, you must consult a physiotherapist or doctor to ensure that there are no physiological problems that may require medical intervention. Due to the nature of the game, there is a great deal of odd movement used in tennis – mainly due to the desire to do whatever it takes to get the ball back over the net. Where you see odd movement patterns, it is important to try to assess how long it takes the individual to re-assert positive movement patterns. The longer it takes, the more likely the movement of the player will seem slower and less effective.

The movement checklists can be used in all areas of the SAQ Continuum, including explosion when resistance equipment is being used. The golden rule is that correct mechanics and form always come first.

RUNNING – STARTING POSITION

Correct	Incorrect	Solution
FEET POSITION ■ Shoulder-width apart	■ Too wide ■ Too close	■ Use chalk marks or marker spots on the surface to indicate best position
■ On the ball of the foot	■ On the toes ■ On the heels ■ Weight outside or inside	■ Lean forwards slightly on the ball of the foot ■ Position feet in a straight line ■ Keep heels off the ground
■ In a straight line	■ Pointing in ■ Splayed out	■ Use straight lines on the ground to position feet ■ Use chalk to mark around the foot on hard surfaces so player can stand in the outline to ensure correct positioning
ARMS ■ Held ready with 90-degree at the elbow ■ One forwards, one back ■ Relaxed	■ Arms by the sides ■ Shoulders shrugged with arms too high ■ Tight and restricted	■ Provide constant feedback on arm technique ■ Practise holding arms in correct position, then accelerate arms as if starting to run – perform Partner arm drive drills (see page 50) ■ Use string looped around index finger and thumb and point of elbow to hold correct position of 90 degrees
HIPS ■ Need to be high or tall and slightly forwards	■ Sunk ■ Twisted	■ Hold head tall and upright ■ Hold stomach in, focus on keeping the hips held high and lean slightly forwards in the direction of running ■ Keep the chin off the chest ■ Focus on a good linear body position
HEAD POSITION ■ Held high ■ Eyes forwards	■ Held down, turned ■ Looking up	■ Imagine you are looking over a fence that comes up to your nose ■ Pick an object in the distance and focus on it

RUNNING – ACCELERATION PHASE

Correct	Incorrect	Solution
HANDS ■ Fingertips gently touching thumb tip	■ Soft (most common) ■ Droopy ■ Tightly closed	■ Hold post-it note or something similar between index finger and thumb
ARM ACTION ■ Fast ■ 90-degree angle at elbow ■ Hand above shoulder ■ One forwards, one back behind hips	■ Slow to medium	■ Perform Partner arm drive drills (see page 50) ■ Use short, sharp sets of on-the-spot fast arm bursts ■ Use light handweights for 8–9 seconds then perform contrast arm drives as quickly as possible afterwards
ARM DRIVE ■ Chin to waist ■ Wrist or hand firm	■ Arms across body ■ Forearm chop ■ At the side ■ Held in a stiff, angled position	■ Perform Partner arm drive drills (see page 50) ■ Brush the inside of the wrist against the waistband, then raise the thumb to touch the chin ■ Use long elastic bands looped between index finger and thumb and elbow, then perform arm drives ■ Perform arm drive drill in front of mirror for feedback ■ Perform Buttock bounces (see page 52)
HEAD ■ Held high ■ Keep up ■ Eyes forwards	■ Held down ■ Turned ■ Looking up ■ Rocking from side to side	■ Imagine you are looking over a fence that comes up to your nose ■ Pick an object in the distance and focus on it
BODY POSITION – TRUNK ■ Tall ■ Strong	■ Sunk ■ Soft ■ Bent	■ Keep the head up; hold the stomach in; keep the hips high, slightly forwards and square
FOOT ACTION ■ Active ■ Plantar flex (toe down) ■ Dorsi flex (toe up)	■ Flat ■ Heel first to touch ground ■ Inactive plantar flex (toe down) and dorsi flex (toe up)	■ Focus on the balls of the feet ■ Remove built-up heeled shoes ■ Practise plantar/dorsi flex skip ■ Ensure there is a slight forward body lean ■ Keep the head up; do not sink into the hips

Contd...

Contd...

Correct	Incorrect	Solution
HEELS ■ Raised	■ Down, contacting ground first	■ Focus on the balls of the feet ■ Remove built-up heeled shoes ■ Roll up cloth or paper and hold with tape into a small ball, slightly larger than a marble. Place in the shoe under the heels
HIPS ■ Tall ■ Square ■ Up/forwards ■ Firm ■ Still	■ Bent ■ Sunk ■ Turned	■ Hold head tall and upright ■ Hold stomach in, focus on keeping the hips held square to the running direction ■ Practise Buttock bounces (see page 52)
KNEES ■ Linear ■ Below waist ■ Foot just off ground ■ Drive forwards	■ Across body ■ Splayed ■ Too high, with foot too high off ground	■ Practise Dead-leg run (see page 53) ■ Teacher/coach to place hands above where knees should lift to; practise bringing the knees up to the hands by running on the spot ■ Use coloured tape; attach from above the knee in a straight line to below knee, either on skin or clothing. The tape should now go across the centre of the kneecap. Now perform on-the-spot running drills in front of a mirror, focusing on keeping the coloured tape in a straight line
RELAXATION ■ Relaxed ■ Calm ■ Comfortable	■ Tense ■ Too loose ■ Distracted	■ Imagine accelerating quickly with power and grace, but staying calm and relaxed ■ Keep breathing controlled

RUNNING – AFTER ACCELERATION (PLANING OUT PHASE)

Correct	Incorrect	Solution
STRIDE LENGTH ▪ Medium for individual	▪ Too long ▪ Too short ▪ Erratic	▪ Use marker spots or stride frequency canes to mark out correct distances of stride length
STRIDE FREQUENCY ▪ Balanced for individual	▪ Too quick ▪ Too slow	▪ Use marker spots or stride frequency canes to mark out correct distances of stride length so that frequency can be determined
ARM ACTION ▪ Fast ▪ 90-degree angle at elbow ▪ Hands above shoulders, behind hips	▪ Slow to medium	▪ Perform Partner arm drive drills (see page 50) ▪ Use short, sharp sets of on-the-spot fast arm bursts ▪ Use light handweights for 8–9 seconds then perform contrast arm drives as quickly as possible afterwards
ARM DRIVE ▪ Chin to waist	▪ Arms across body ▪ Forearm chopping ▪ Arms at the sides ▪ Arms held in stiff angled position	▪ Perform Partner arm drive drills (see page 50) ▪ Brush the inside of the wrist against the waistband, then thumb rises to touch the chin ▪ Loop long elastic bands between index finger and thumb and around the elbow, then perform arm drives ▪ Perform arm drive drill in front of a mirror for feedback ▪ Perform Buttock bounces (see page 52)
HEAD ▪ Held high ▪ Keep up ▪ Eyes forwards	▪ Held down ▪ Turned ▪ Looking up ▪ Rocking from side to side	▪ Imagine you are looking over a fence that comes up to your nose ▪ Pick an object in the distance and focus on it
BODY POSITION – TRUNK ▪ Tall	▪ Sunk ▪ Soft ▪ Bent	▪ Hold head up; hold stomach in, with the hips high, slightly forwards and square

Contd...

Contd...

Correct	Incorrect	Solution
FOOT ACTION ■ Active ■ Plantar flex (toe down) ■ Dorsi flex (toe up)	■ Flat ■ Heel first to touch ground ■ Inactive plantar (toe down) /dorsi (toe up) flex	■ Focus on the balls of the feet ■ Remove built-up heeled shoes ■ Practise plantar/dorsi flex skip ■ Ensure there is a slight forward body lean ■ Keep head up; do not sink into the hips
RELAXATION ■ Relaxed ■ Calm ■ Comfortable	■ Tense ■ Too loose ■ Distracted	■ Imagine accelerating quickly with power and grace, but remaining calm and relaxed ■ Breathing to be controlled

LATERAL STEPPING

Correct	Incorrect	Solution
FOOT ACTION ■ Work off balls of the feet	■ On the heels ■ Flat footed	■ Lean slightly forwards even when stepping sideways ■ Provide constant feedback to keep off the heels ■ Keep hips tall and strong; this helps control power and prevent flat-footed weight transfer
■ Feet shoulder-width apart	■ Too wide ■ Too close ■ Crossed ■ Pointing in ■ Splayed out	■ Use marker spots to indicate best foot position for lateral stepping ■ Practise stepping slowly at first, then build up speed gradually
■ Drive off the trailing foot	■ Reach with leading foot ■ Flat-footed ■ On heels ■ Feet pointing in or splayed	■ Use marker spots to indicate best foot positions ■ Attach coloured tape from tongue to end of shoes in a straight line, then work in front of a mirror, focusing on keeping the lines on the feet straight ■ Tape a ball of paper under the heel of each foot ■ Use angled boards to step off

Contd...

Contd...

Correct	Incorrect	Solution
HIPS ■ Firm ■ Controlled ■ Square ■ High	■ Soft ■ Twisted ■ Angled ■ Leaning too far forwards ■ Bent at the waist ■ Sunk	■ Hold head tall ■ Hold stomach in ■ Focus on keeping the hips square
ARMS ■ 90-degree arm drive ■ Fast and strong drive	■ Arms going across the body ■ No arm drive at all ■ Arms too tight and restricted ■ Arms moving forwards but not driving backwards behind the hips	■ Perform Partner arm drive drills (see page 50) and practise moving sideways ■ Perform Mirror drills (see page 51) ■ Provide constant positive feedback
TRUNK ■ Strong and firm ■ Slight lean forwards	■ Too upright ■ Leaning too far forwards ■ Bent at the waist ■ Leaning back	■ Perform Mirror drills (see page 51) ■ Keep head looking forwards and still ■ Hold stomach in ■ Slight knee bend only

LATERAL TURNING – 90 DEGREES

Correct	Incorrect	Solution
FEET ■ Shoulder-width apart	■ Together ■ Too wide ■ Crossed	■ Use chalk marks or marker spots to indicate best starting and finishing position
ON THE TURN ■ Feet stay shoulder-width apart ■ Work on the balls of the feet	■ Come together ■ Cross ■ Go apart too wide ■ Go onto heels ■ Go onto toes	■ Use chalk marks or marker spots to indicate best starting and finishing position ■ Practise single turn in front of a mirror
FOOT DRIVE ■ Drive off trailing foot	■ Forward reach ■ Jump on the spot ■ Rock back on heels	■ Keep trunk firm ■ Get individuals to say the word 'push' on the drive and 'off' on the turn, either on their heads or out loud ■ Practise lateral side-steps slowly then gradually build up speed ■ Maintain good arm drive
HIPS ■ High, slightly forwards and square ■ Hip before knee	■ Hips low and sunk ■ Angled, not square ■ Trunk leaning too far forwards or too upright	■ Keep hips firm, tall and leaning forwards ■ Use arm drive with hips to assist turn ■ Keep hips square when turning ■ Practise turns slowly at first
HEAD ■ Keep up ■ Off the chest ■ Eyes looking forwards ■ Head and hips work simultaneously during turn	■ Floppy ■ Down ■ Angled ■ Back	■ Pick two distant objects, one in front of you, the other in the direction you are turning to. Initially focus on the object in front, then on the turn refocus onto the second object

180–DEGREE TURN

Correct	Incorrect	Solution
INITIAL MOVEMENT ■ Seamless ■ Movement smooth, no punctuations ■ Sequence is drop, step and go (1–2–3)	■ Jumping up ■ Stepping back ■ Twisting	■ Practise drop step, the opening of the leg to point in the direction of the turn; the trailing foot then pushes off ■ Practise saying out loud, 'drop, step and go' ■ Practise slowly at first, gradually developing speed ■ Practise facing a wall, so when you turn the back step is prevented ■ Practise in front of a mirror ■ Use a video of the turn
FEET ■ Shoulder-width apart	■ Together ■ Too wide ■ Crossed	■ Use chalk marks or marker spots to indicate best starting and finishing position
ARM DRIVE ■ 90-degree arm drive, same as for lateral turn ■ Fast and strong drive	■ Arms going across the body ■ No arm drive at all ■ Arms too tight and restricted ■ Arms moving forwards but not driving backwards behind the hips	■ Perform Partner arm drive drills (see page 50), practise moving sideways. ■ Perform Mirror drills (see page 51) ■ Provide constant positive feedback
HEAD ■ Up ■ Eyes looking forwards	■ Down ■ Angled ■ Turned	■ Pick two distant objects, one in front of you, the other behind. Initially focus on the object in front, then on the turn refocus onto the second object (behind)
HIPS ■ High, slightly forwards and square ■ Hips before knees	■ Hips low and sunk ■ Angled not square ■ Trunk leaning too far forwards or too upright	■ Keep hips firm, tall and leaning forwards ■ Use arm drive with hips to assist turn ■ Hips kept square when turning ■ Practise turns slowly at first

JUMPING

Correct	Incorrect	Solution
ARM DRIVE ■ Arms at 90-degree angle at the elbows, working together from behind the hips to above the head	■ No arm movement ■ Arms not working together ■ One arm used	■ Practise with a balloon. Hold the balloon in front, below the chest, with both hands, then throw it over the back of the head ■ Once the balloon drill has been perfected, introduce the throwing of the balloon with a jump ■ Demonstrate the difference between jumping with and without arm drive. Attempt a jump with arms at the sides then repeat with positive arm action
PRE-JUMP HIPS ■ Tall, slightly forwards	■ Bent ■ Sunk (most common)	■ Keep hips firm, tall and leaning forwards ■ Keep hips square when jumping ■ Keep head up, and hold stomach in
TAKE OFF FEET ■ On the balls of the feet	■ Flatfooted ■ On the heels ■ On the toes	■ Provide constant feedback to keep off heels ■ Keep hips tall and strong; this helps control power and prevent flat-footed weight transfer ■ Use a small round stick or old books half an inch thick. Place under both heels so that weight is forced onto the balls of the feet. Practise jumping in this position
LANDING ■ On the balls of the feet ■ Weight equally balanced on both feet when possible	■ On the toes ■ On the heels ■ Unbalanced	■ Practise multiple bunny hops, landing on the balls of the feet, so that correct foot-to-ground contact is practised ■ Place taped ball of paper (the size of a marble) under the heel of each foot ■ Draw small circles or use small marker spots 2–3 inches in diameter as landing markers for the balls of the feet
TRUNK ■ Tall, hips leaning slightly forwards ■ Firm and relaxed	■ Sunk ■ Bent at the waist ■ Twisted ■ Uncontrolled	■ Breathe in and hold the stomach firm; keep the head high.

Contd...

Contd...

Correct	Incorrect	Solution
HIPS ■ Firm ■ Tall ■ Leaning slightly forwards	■ Hips low and sunk ■ Angled, not square ■ Trunk leaning too far forwards or too upright	■ Keep hips firm, tall and leaning forwards ■ Use arm drive with hips to assist control ■ Keep hips square when landing ■ Practise landing by simply jumping off a step or small box ■ Imagine perfect body position

DECELERATION

Correct	Incorrect	Solution
ARMS ■ 90-degree angle at elbows ■ Increase speed of drive on deceleration	■ Slow arm drive ■ No arm drive ■ Arms dropped by the sides	■ Provide feedback of 'drive arms' as soon as deceleration commences ■ Use string or elastic bands looped around index finger and thumb and point of elbow to hold correct position of 90 degrees ■ Use light handweights that are released on the deceleration phase
FEET ■ Shorten stride to smaller steps	■ Maintain long strides	■ Use coloured canes, marker dots or a short piece of outdoor Fast Foot Ladder on the deceleration phase
HEAD ■ Slightly raised above the horizontal plane ■ Eyes up	■ Chin down on chest ■ Head turned to one side	■ Prior to deceleration phase, pick an object in the distance that is slightly higher than the horizon, therefore requiring the head to be brought up ■ Coach to call 'head up' as deceleration phase begins
HIPS ■ Lean back	■ Remaining forwards ■ Lop-sided ■ Sunk	■ Focus on the head being brought up; this will change the angle of the hips

Contd...

Contd...

TRUNK		
■ Brought upright	■ Remaining tilted forwards ■ Bent	■ Get player to focus on: 1. Head up 2. Trunk up 3. Hips back Work on this combination during deceleration.

HEELS
■ Weight transferred
   to heel
■ Heel first
	■ On the toes
	■ Too much weight forwards
	   on the balls of the feet
		■ Get athlete to focus on:
		1. Head up
		2. Trunk up
		3. Hips back
		Work on this combination during deceleration. This will also impact on the spine and transfer to the heel coming down to the ground first for deceleration

Tennis–specific mechanics

In tennis certain movements are used to ensure that the player has ideal contact with the racket and ball. Many of the movement patterns are performed automatically using anticipation and muscle memory. Due to the nature of tennis and the player's desire to get to the ball and return it at all costs, a player will execute odd non-mechanically sound movements such as landing on the heel of the foot. Tennis players are not marathon runners, as already highlighted in movement analysis research featured in this book; all of their movements are short in length and duration. Sprinters have spikes on the balls of their feet for power generation and all power sports including football, rugby, basketball and American football, where explosive speed is paramount, acknowledge that generating power from the ball of the foot is essential. Recent research by Nike in regard to the development of the Nike Free running shoe discovered that African marathon runners ran with their feet in a neutral to the ball of the foot position, not heel to toe. Not only does running on the heel cause deceleration, it also physiologically prevents the efficient dispersion of energy, resulting in lower limb injuries. We also have to take into account technological advances in training shoes where shoe heels have been built up more for comfort and fashion than for actually promoting explosive running. The Nike Free research also discovered that African barefoot marathon runners rarely have foot, heel, ankle and knee injuries (Nike Sports Research Lab, 2004).

Below is a checklist of terminology used in describing tennis-specific movements. A high percentage of movement used on the court is basic mechanics described in the fundamental movement checklists. It is recommended that after players have executed a tennis-specific mechanical movement they should be encouraged to revert to standard mechanical movements as soon as possible prior to executing the next tennis-specific movement. This will ensure maximum efficiency and economics on the court, therefore the player will move more quickly and faster.

TENNIS-SPECIFIC MECHANICS CHECKLIST

Movement	Description
DYNAMIC BALANCE	Ability to maintain centre of gravity over lower support base while body is moving
FORWARD STEP	Moving forwards, transferring power through the balls of the feet
SPLIT STEP	Returning to the surface after both feet have been off the ground. The foot farthest away from the ball should land first, just before the other foot
STAB/JAB STEP	Lead foot steps first towards the direction of the ball
SIDE-STEP	Lateral movement using short, explosive steps, keeping the hips square; feet do not cross over
SHUFFLE STEP	Lateral movement using very short, explosive steps, keeping the hips square; feet do not cross over
PIVOT STEP	Turning the hips towards the ball while pivoting the lead foot, with the first step being made by the foot furthest from the ball
CROSS-OVER STEP	Lateral step with one leg crossing over the other
LUNGE STEP	Extending forwards with the lead foot, widening the base to enable an extended lunge forwards
DROP STEP	Seamless opening of the leg to point in the direction of turn; trailing foot then pushes off

DRILL ARM MECHANICS – PARTNER DRILLS

Aim
To perfect the correct arm technique for running in tennis.

Area/equipment
The player works with a partner.

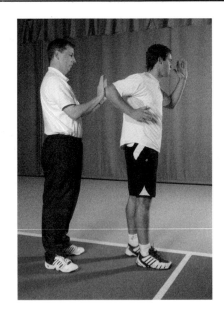

Description
Player stands with a partner behind him/her. The partner holds the palms of his/her hands in line with the player's elbows, fingers pointing upwards. The player fires the arms as if sprinting so that the elbows smack into the partner's palms.

Key teaching points
- Arms should not move across the body
- Elbows should be at a 90-degree angle
- Hands and shoulders should be relaxed
- The insides of the wrists should brush against the hips
- Ensure that the player performs a full ROM – the hands should move from the buttock cheeks to the chest or head
- Encourage speed of movement to hear the smack

Sets and reps
3 sets of 16 reps with a 1-minute recovery between each set.

Variations/progressions
- Use light handweights for the first two sets, then perform the last set without
- Perform the drill while holding a racket

DRILL ARM MECHANICS – MIRROR DRILLS

Aim
To perfect the correct arm technique for running in tennis.

Area/equipment
A large mirror.

Description
Player stands in front of the mirror with his/her arms ready for sprinting and performs short bursts of arm drives. Use the mirror as a feedback tool to perfect the technique.

Key teaching points
- Arms should not move across the body
- Elbows should be at a 90-degree angle
- Hands and shoulders should be relaxed
- The insides of the wrists should brush against the hips
- Ensure that the player performs a full ROM – the hands should move from the buttock cheeks to the chest or head

Sets and reps
3 sets of 16 reps with a 1-minute recovery between each set.

Variations/progressions
- Use light handweights for the first two sets, then perform the last set without
- Perform the drill while holding a racket

DRILL   ARM MECHANICS – BUTTOCK BOUNCES

Aim
To develop an explosive arm drive.

Area/equipment
A suitable ground surface.

Description
Player sits on the floor with his/her legs straight out in front and fires the arms rapidly in short bursts. The power generated should be great enough to raise the buttocks off the floor in a bouncing manner.

Key teaching points
- Arms should not move across the body
- Elbows should be at a 90-degree angle
- Hands and shoulders should be relaxed
- The insides of the wrists should brush against the hips
- Ensure that the player performs a full ROM – the hands should move from the buttock cheeks to the chest or head
- Encourage speed of movement to hear the smack

Sets and reps
3 sets of 6 reps; each rep is 6–8 explosive arm drives with a 1-minute recovery between each set.

Variations/progressions
- Use light handweights for the first 2 sets, then perform the last set without
- Perform the drill while holding a racket

DRILL RUNNING FORM – DEAD-LEG RUN

Aim
To develop a quick knee lift and the positive foot placement required for effective sprinting.

Area/equipment
Indoor or outdoor area. Using hurdles, markers or sticks, place approximately 8 obstacles in a straight line at 2-foot intervals. Place a marker 1 yard from each end of the line to mark the start and finish.

Description
Player must keep the outside leg straight in a locked position. The inside leg moves over the obstacles in a cycling motion while the outside leg swings along just above the ground. See Fig. 2.2.

Key teaching points
- Bring the knee of the inside leg up to just below 90 degrees
- Point the toe upwards
- Bring the inside leg back down quickly between the hurdles
- Increase the speed of the movement once the technique has been mastered
- Maintain correct arm mechanics
- Maintain an upright posture and a strong core
- Keep the hips square and stand tall

Sets and reps
1 set of 6 reps, 3 leading with the left leg and 3 with the right.

Variations/progressions
- Use light handweights – accelerate off the end of the last obstacle and drop the handweights during this acceleration phase
- Place several different-coloured markers 2 yards from the last hurdle at different angles. As the player leaves the last hurdle, the coach nominates a marker for the player to accelerate on to
- Perform the drill while holding a racket

Figure 2.2 Dead-leg run

DRILL   RUNNING FORM – PRE-TURN

Aim
To educate and prepare the hips, legs and feet for effective and quick turning without fully committing the whole body; to maintain dynamic balance, keeping the centre of gravity over the base of support while the body is moving.

Area/equipment
Indoor or outdoor area. Using hurdles, markers or sticks, place about 8 obstacles in a straight line at 2-foot intervals. Place a marker 1 yard from each end of the line to mark the start and finish.

Description
Player moves sideways along the line of obstacles, just in front of them (i.e. not travelling over them). The back leg (following leg) is brought over the hurdle to a position slightly in front of the body so that the heel is in line with the toe of the leading foot. As the back foot is planted, the leading foot moves away. Repeat the drill with the opposite leg leading. See Fig. 2.3.

Key teaching points
- Stand tall and do not sink into the hips
- Do not allow the feet to cross over
- Keep the feet shoulder-width apart as much as possible
- The knee lift should be no greater than 45 degrees
- Maintain correct arm mechanics
- Maintain an upright posture
- Keep the hips and shoulders square
- Work both the left and right sides

Sets and reps
1 set of 6 reps, 3 leading with the left shoulder and 3 leading with the right.

Variations/progressions
- Use light handweights – at the end of the obstacles, turn and accelerate 5 yards. Drop the weights halfway through the acceleration phase
- Place several different-coloured markers 2 yards from the last hurdle at different angles. As the player leaves the last hurdle, the coach nominates a marker for the player to accelerate to
- Partner stands 2 yards from the first hurdle with a ball held out in each hand above the shoulders. As the player leaves the last hurdle, the partner drops one of the balls. The player accelerates to catch the ball or hit it with a racket on the second bounce

Figure 2.3 Pre-turn

DRILL RUNNING FORM – LEADING LEG RUN

Aim
To develop quick, efficient steps and running techniques.

Area/equipment
Indoor or outdoor area. Using hurdles, markers or sticks, place approximately 8 obstacles in a straight line at 2-foot intervals. Place a marker 1 yard from each end of the line to mark the start and finish.

Description
Player runs down the line of obstacles, crossing over each one with the same lead leg. The aim is to just clear the obstacles. Repeat the drill using the opposite leg as the lead. See Fig. 2.4.

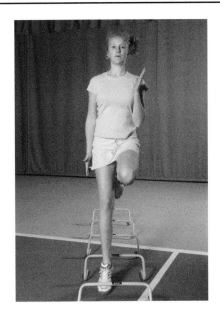

Key teaching points
- The knee lift should be no more than 45 degrees
- Use short, sharp steps
- Maintain strong arm mechanics
- Maintain an upright posture
- Stand tall and do not sink into the hips

Sets and reps
1 set of 6 reps, 3 leading with the left leg and 3 leading with the right.

Variations/progressions
- Perform the drill while holding a racket
- To practise changing direction after running in a straight line, place 3 markers 2–3 yards away from the end of the obstacles at different angles; on leaving the last obstacle, the player sprints out to the marker nominated by the coach
- Vary the distance between the hurdles to achieve different stride lengths
- On leaving the last obstacle, the player moves to return a ball played from the coach standing various distances away

Figure 2.4 Leading leg run

RUNNING FORM –
DRILL   QUICK SIDE-STEP DEVELOPMENT

Aim
To develop correct, precise and controlled recovery steps (side-step or shuffle); to maintain dynamic balance, keeping the centre of gravity over the base of support while the body is moving.

Area/equipment
Indoor or outdoor area. Place 3 hurdles side by side about 18 inches apart.

Description
Player stands on the outside of hurdle 1 so that he/she will step over the middle of each hurdle. The player performs lateral movement mechanics while clearing each hurdle. On clearing hurdle 3, he/she repeats the drill in the opposite direction.

Key teaching points
- Maintain correct lateral running form/mechanics
- Maintain correct arm mechanics
- Do not sink into the hips
- Keep the head up
- Do not lean too far forwards
- Use small steps and work off the balls of the feet
- Do not use an excessively high knee lift

Sets and reps
2 sets of 10 reps, 5 to the left and 5 to the right with a 60-second recovery between sets.

Variations/progressions
- Work with a coach or a partner who should randomly direct the player over the hurdles
- Work with a coach or a partner who randomly directs the player over the hurdles, at the same time hitting the ball for the player to return (see Fig. 2.5 (a))
- Add 2 Macro V Hurdles to add lift variations
- Work in groups of 3 players: player 1 works through the hurdles; players 2 and 3 stand at either end and hit a ball for player 1 to return as he/she gets to their end (see Fig. 2.5 (b))
- Players 2 and 3 stand at opposite ends and opposite sides of the hurdles. Player 1 works through the hurdles, receiving and returning the ball from Player 2. On stepping over the last hurdle, player 1 uses pivot step turns and receives and returns the ball from Player 3, then works back down the hurdles facing in the other direction, repeats the pivot step at the end and continues the drill (see Fig. 2.5 (c))

Figure 2.5(a) Quick side-step
development – variation 1

RUNNING FORM –
QUICK SIDE-STEP DEVELOPMENT (Contd...)

Figure 2.5(b) Quick side-step development – variation 2

Figure 2.5(c) Quick side-step development – variation 3

DRILL
RUNNING FORM –
LATERAL STEP/SHUFFLE DEVELOPMENT

Aim
To develop efficient and economical lateral side-steps and shuffle when receiving and returning a tennis ball.

Area/equipment
Half a tennis court or an indoor or outdoor grid 13 yards in length. Tennis racket and tennis balls. Place 8 Micro V Hurdles side on, 1 yard apart and staggered laterally. Position a finish marker dot in the same pattern as the hurdles.

Description
Player 1 works inside the channel created by the hurdles, stepping over each hurdle with one foot as he/she moves laterally down and across the channel. On stepping over the outside hurdle, a ball is hit or thrown to him/her, to be returned to player 2 who is situated on that side of the hurdles. This action is then repeated on the opposite side with player 3. After receiving the ball, players 2 and 3 walk backwards into position ready for the next time player 1 steps over the outside hurdle. See Fig. 2.6.

Key teaching points
- Bring the knee up to a 45-degree angle over the hurdle
- Do not 'over-stride' across the hurdle
- Maintain correct arm mechanics and a strong arm drive
- Keep the hips square
- Do not sink into the hips

Sets and reps
2 sets of 3 reps with a walk-back recovery between reps and a 2-minute recovery between sets.

Variation/progression
Perform the drill backwards.

Figure 2.6 Lateral step/shuffle development

DRILL

RUNNING FORM –
LATERAL/SHUFFLE STEP

Aim

To develop efficient and economical lateral/shuffle steps; to maintain dynamic balance; to develop efficient movement while holding a tennis racket.

Area/equipment

Indoor or outdoor area. Using hurdles, markers or sticks, place approximately 8 obstacles in a straight line at 2-foot intervals. Place a marker 1 yard from each end of the line to mark the start and finish.

Description

Player steps over each obstacle, moving sideways. See Fig. 2.7.

Key teaching points

- Bring the knee up to just below 45 degrees
- Do not skip sideways – step!
- Push off from the back foot
- Do not pull with the lead foot
- Maintain correct arm mechanics
- Maintain an upright posture
- Keep the hips square
- Do not sink into the hips

Sets and reps

1 set of 6 reps, 3 leading with the left shoulder and 3 leading with the right.

Variations/progressions

- Use light handweights – after the last obstacle, perform a pivot step, drop the handweights and accelerate off in the direction you are facing
- Place several different-coloured markers 2 yards from the last hurdle. As the player leaves the last hurdle, the coach nominates a marker for the player to accelerate to and return a ball thrown to them by the coach
- The drill can be performed with the player juggling a ball with his/her racket, using either side of strings and frame

Figure 2.7   Lateral/shuffle step

DRILL RUNNING FORM – 1–2–3 LIFT

Aim
To develop an efficient leg cycle, rhythm, power, foot placement and dynamic balance.

Area/equipment
Indoor or outdoor area 30–40 yards in length. Tennis racket.

Description
Player moves in a straight line; after every third step, the leg is brought up in an explosive action so that the knee is at a 90-degree angle. Continue the drill over the length prescribed, working the same leg, then repeat the drill leading with the other leg. See Fig. 2.8.

Key teaching points
- Keep the hips square
- Work off the balls of the feet
- Try to develop and maintain a rhythm
- Keep the eyes and head up and look ahead
- Maintain correct arm mechanics
- Maintain an upright posture
- Leg to be snapped quickly up and down

Sets and reps
1 set of 6 reps, 3 leading with the left leg and 3 leading with the right.

Variations/progressions
- Alternate the lead leg during a repetition
- Vary the lift sequence, e.g. 1–2–3–4 lift, etc.
- At the end of the run, coach can hit a ball for the player to return

Figure 2.8 1–2–3 lift

DRILL   *JUMPING – SINGLE JUMPS*

Aim
To develop jumping techniques, power, speed, control and dynamic balance.

Area/equipment
Indoor or outdoor area. Tennis racket. Ensure the surface is clear of any obstacles. Use a 7- or 12-inch hurdle.

Description
Player jumps over a single hurdle and, on landing, walks back to the start point to repeat the drill. See Fig. 2.9(a).

Key teaching points
- Maintain good arm mechanics
- Do not sink into the hips at the take-off and landing phases
- Land on the balls of the feet
- Do not fall back on the heels

Sets and reps
2 sets of 8 reps with a 1-minute recovery between each set.

Variations/progressions
- Perform single jumps over the hurdle and back
- Perform single jumps over the hurdle with a 180-degree twist; practise twisting to both sides (see Fig. 2.9(b))
- Perform lateral single jumps – jump from both sides (see Fig. 2.9(c))
- A ball can be thrown to the player for him/her to return on landing

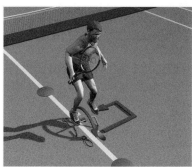

Figure 2.9(a) Single jump

Figure 2.9(b) Single jump with
180-degree twist

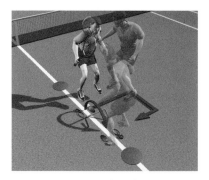

Figure 2.9(c) Lateral single jump

DRILL   *MULTIPLE HOPS AND JUMPS*

Aim
To develop maximum control while taking off and landing; to develop controlled directional power and dynamic balance.

Area/equipment
Indoor or outdoor area. Tennis racket. Place six to eight 7- or 12-inch hurdles at 2-foot intervals in a straight line.

Description
Player jumps forwards over each hurdle in quick succession until all the hurdles have been cleared, then walks back to the start and repeats the drill.

Key teaching points
- Use quick, rhythmic arm mechanics
- Do not sink into the hips at the take-off and landing phases
- Land and take off on the balls of the feet
- Stand tall and look straight ahead
- Maintain control
- Start slowly and gradually build up the speed

Sets and reps
2 sets of 6 reps with a 1-minute recovery between each set.

Variations/progressions
- Perform lateral jumps (see Fig. 2.10(a))
- Perform jumps with a 180-degree twist (see Fig. 2.10(b))
- Hop over the hurdles, balance, then repeat (see Fig. 2.10(c))
- Use light handweights – for the last rep of each of the sets, perform the drill without the weights as a contrast
- Perform two forward jumps and one back

MULTIPLE HOPS AND JUMPS (Contd...)

Figure 2.10(a) Lateral jumps

Figure 2.10(b) Jumps with 180-degree twist

Figure 2.10(c) Hops

DRILL
STRIDE FREQUENCY AND LENGTH

Aim

To practise the transfer from the acceleration phase to the increase in stride frequency and length required when running; to develop an efficient leg cycle, rhythm, power, foot placement, deceleration, control and balance while moving over longer distances on the tennis court (for example when getting to a drop shot from 2–3 yards behind the base line).

Area/equipment

Indoor or outdoor area at least 30 yards square. If you are using a tennis court, the drill will start 3–4 yards behind the base line and finish 2.5 feet before the net line. Place 15 coloured stride frequency canes, marker dots or sticks at different intervals flat on the ground in a straight line. See Fig. 2.11.

Description

Player starts from behind the base line and accelerates over the first canes. The canes are laid out so that the initial stages of the run develop acceleration, therefore they are closer together; in the middle part the canes are wider apart, to develop stride length; and the final few canes are closer together again to develop deceleration.

Key teaching points

- Do not over-stride
- Work off the balls of the feet
- Try to develop and maintain a rhythm
- Keep the eyes and head up as if you are looking over a fence
- Maintain correct running mechanics
- Maintain an upright posture
- Stay focused
- Alter distances between strides for different ages and heights

Sets and reps

1 set of 4 reps.

Variations/progressions

- Work with a partner, who delivers drop shots in between the final cane and the net for the player to accelerate on to and return the ball
- Work with a partner who delivers a drop shot; on reaching the drop shot the partner lobs a ball behind the base line and the player turns and repeats the stride frequency drill back down the canes to return the second ball

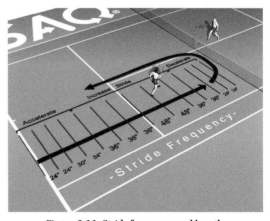

Figure 2.11 Stride frequency and length

RUNNING FORM –
DRILL   STRIDE FREQUENCY AND LENGTH (ADVANCED

Aim

To practise the transfer from the acceleration phase to the increase in stride frequency and length required when running; to develop an efficient leg cycle, rhythm, power, foot placement, deceleration, control and balance while competing against an opponent.

Area/equipment

Indoor or outdoor area at least 30 yards square. If you are using a tennis court, the drill will start 3–4 yards behind the base line and finish 2.5 feet before the net line. Place 15 coloured stride frequency canes, marker dots or sticks at different intervals flat on the ground in a straight line. Repeat the layout on the other side of the court or 2–3 yards to the side. See Fig. 2.12.

Description

Two players start from behind the base line and accelerate over the grid, competing against each other over the first canes. The canes are laid out so that the initial stages for the run develop acceleration, therefore they are closer together; the middle canes are wider apart, to develop stride length; and the final few canes are closer together again to develop deceleration. The winner is the player who clears the final cane first.

Key teaching points

- Do not over-stride
- Work off the balls of the feet
- Try to develop and maintain a rhythm
- Keep the eyes and head up as if looking over a fence
- Maintain correct mechanics
- Maintain an upright posture
- Stay focused
- Alter distances between strides for different ages and heights

Sets and reps

1 set of 4 reps.

Variation/progression

Introduce 'out and back' run; the winner is the player who returns to the start first. This is a great drill for developing a quick turn near the net.

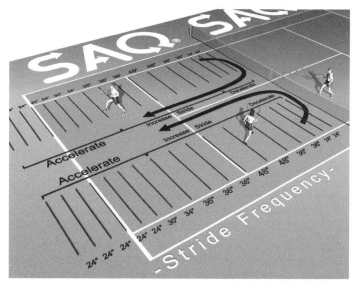

Figure 2.12 Stride frequency and length (advanced)

DRILL RUNNING FORM – WITH BALL RETURN

Aim
To maintain good mechanics, balance and co-ordination while moving into position to play a stroke; to improve decision-making ability.

Area/equipment
Indoor or outdoor area. Tennis balls. Place 8 hurdles in a straight line at 2-foot intervals. Place the first marker dot at one end and a second marker dot at the other end, approximately 2 yards away from the last hurdle.

Description
The coach or partner stands just behind the second marker dot (34 yards away). The player performs a mechanics drill through the hurdles and, on clearing the final hurdle, accelerates onto the ball that has been thrown or served at an angle away from the second marker dot. The player returns the ball to the coach/partner, then turns and accelerates back to the base line. See Fig. 2.13.

Key teaching points
- Maintain correct mechanics
- Stay focused by looking ahead
- Fire the arms explosively when accelerating to the tennis ball

Sets and reps
3 sets of 6 reps. NB: the sets should be made up of various mechanics drills.

Variations/progressions
- On clearing the final hurdle, the ball is served or thrown at various heights into the air for the player to return
- The player performs lateral mechanics drills, and on clearing the last hurdle will turn onto the ball

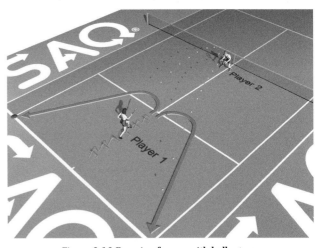

Figure 2.13 Running form – with ball return

DRILL
RUNNING FORM –
HURDLE MIRROR DRILLS

Aim
To improve the performance of mechanics under pressure; to improve random agility, dynamic balance and co-ordination.

Area/equipment
Half a tennis court or an indoor or outdoor grid 13 yards in length. Tennis racket and tennis balls. Mark out a grid with 2 lines of 8 hurdles, with 2 feet between each hurdle and 2 yards between each line of hurdles.

Description
Players face each other while performing mechanics drills up and down the lines of hurdles. One player initiates the movements while the partner attempts to mirror those movements. The lead player can perform both lateral and linear mirror drills. See Fig. 2.14(a).

Key teaching points
■ Stay focused on your partner
■ The player mirroring should try to anticipate the lead player's movements
■ Maintain correct arm mechanics while holding the racket

Sets and reps
Each player performs 3 sets of 30-second work periods, with a 30-second recovery between each work period.

Variations/progressions
■ Players to perform drills while controlling a tennis ball with their racket
■ Perform lateral drills as above with the players working in pairs with only 2 hurdles per player; this will improve short-stepping and the lateral steps used pre-ball strike. See Fig. 2.14(b).

Figure 2.14(a) Hurdle mirror drill

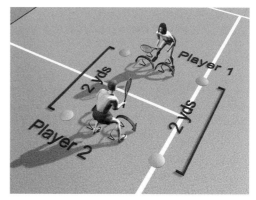

Figure 2.14(b) Hurdle mirror drill – variation

DRILL RUNNING FORM – CURVED ANGLE RUN

Aim
To develop controlled, explosive fast feet while running on a curved angle.

Area/equipment
Half a tennis court or an indoor or outdoor grid 13 yards in length. Tennis racket and tennis balls. Place 10 hurdles in a curved formation, 2 feet apart. Place a marker at each end, approximately 2 yards from the first and last hurdles respectively.

Description
Player performs running drills through the hurdles, such as the Dead-leg run (page 53), Lateral stepping (page 59) or Leading leg run (page 55). See Fig. 2.15.

Key teaching points
- Work both left and right sides
- The knee lift should be no more than 45 degrees
- Use short, sharp steps
- Maintain powerful arm mechanics
- Maintain an upright posture
- Look ahead at all times

Sets and reps
Each player performs 1 set of 6 reps with a 30-second recovery between each rep.

Variations/progressions
- Introduce a tennis ball for the player to return while performing the drill or run on to at the end of the drill
- Introduce tighter curves
- Use immediately after straight run hurdle work

Figure 2.15 Curved angle run

DRILL   RUNNING FORM – COMPLEX MECHANICS

Aim

To prevent players reverting to bad habits, particularly when under pressure; to challenge players by placing them in match-like pressure situations; to maintain good running form even in the most difficult and demanding of situations.

Area/equipment

Half a tennis court or an indoor or outdoor grid 13 yards in length. Tennis racket and tennis balls. Place 4 hurdles in a straight line with 2 feet between each hurdle. The next 4 hurdles are set slightly to one side and the final 4 hurdles are placed back in line with the original 4. See Fig. 2.16(a).

Description

Player performs a dead-leg run over the hurdles with the dead leg changing over the 4 centre hurdles. Return to the start by performing the drill over the hurdles in the opposite direction.

Figure 2.16(a) Complex mechanics

Key teaching points

- Maintain correct arm mechanics
- Work off the balls of the feet
- Try to develop and maintain a rhythm
- Keep the eyes and head up and look ahead
- Maintain an upright posture
- Keep the hips square

Sets and reps

4 sets of 4 reps.

Variations/progressions

- Perform the drill laterally, moving both forwards and backwards to cross the centre 4 hurdles. See Fig. 2.16(b)
- Place the hurdles in a cross formation and perform drills up to the centre and sideways, left or right, up or across
- Introduce players from other sides/groups
- When the drill has been mastered, players can accelerate out of the last hurdle onto a tennis ball that they must return

Figure 2.16(b) Complex lateral mechanics

Tennis–specific endurance

Tennis, as already described in this book, is a multi-directional, explosive, stop–start activity, with 80 per cent of all base line strokes on clay courts performed with a player moving less than 3 metres (Ferrauti et al., 2002). Other research has highlighted the fact that performing long, slow runs to develop endurance will have a negative impact on anaerobic performance. This is mainly due to the fact that long, slow running changes the muscle fibre type recruited: the performance of long-distance, low-intensity exercise will result in the recruitment of aerobic slow-twitch muscle fibres. This leads to an increase in metabolic and neural fatigue, which will inhibit a player's ability to recruit the fast-twitch anaerobic muscle fibres necessary to perform the explosive movements that dominate the game of tennis. Research has suggested that a 'couch potato' – a person who is sedentary – possesses more fast-twitch muscle fibres than a middle- to long-distance athlete. In addition, long, slow running in one direction does not represent in any shape or form the movement demands placed upon a tennis player during a game. A more appropriate and effective approach to developing tennis-specific endurance is the use of intensive interval training in which rest, recovery and movement patterns can be designed and manipulated to achieve greater levels of endurance. Remember, if you train slow you will play slow.

DRILL
RUNNING FORM –
CLOCK ENDURANCE RUNS

Aim
To develop tennis-specific speed endurance.

Area/equipment
Half a tennis court or an indoor or outdoor grid 13 yards in length. Tennis racket. 9 marker dots. Place 8 marker dots in a 12-yard square and the remaining marker dot in the middle of the square. See Fig. 2.17.

Description
The centre dot is given the letter A. The other marker dots are placed approximately 6 yards from the centre marker dot in a clock formation. The forward marker dot will be 12 o'clock, forward right marker dot is 1:30, right marker dot is 3 o'clock, back right marker dot is 4:30, back marker dot is 6 o'clock, back left marker dot is 7:30, left marker dot is 9 o'clock and forward left marker dot is 10:30.

Player performs interval runs as outlined below. For example, in the first set the player runs from A to 12:00, 12:00 to 10:30 and 10:30 to A. This run equals approximately 18 yards. This equals 1 rep; 1 set of 5 reps equals 90 yards. The second set could be A to 6:00, 6:00 to 4:30, 4:30 to 1:30, 1:30 to A, A to 9:00, 9:00 to A. This rep is 42 yards; 1 set of 5 reps equals 210 yards.

Work:rest ratio (recovery between runs)
The work:rest ratio between each run will be as follows: 1:3, 1:2, etc. This means that if the run takes 8 seconds, the rest period will be either 3 or 2 times longer, i.e. 24 or 16 seconds. These times can be varied to increase the intensity of the work.

Recovery between sets
This is the recovery time between each set of runs.

Interval runs

Set one
5 × A to 12:00, 12:00 to 10:30, 10:30 to 9:00, 9:00 to A
Work:rest ratio: 1:3 pre-season, 1:2 in season
Recovery between sets: 2 minutes
Total distance: 120 yards

Set two
5 × A to 6:00, 6:00 to 7:30, 7:30 to 4:30, 4:30 to A, A to 12:00, 12:00 to A
Work:rest ratio: 1:3 pre-season, 1:2 in season
Recovery between sets: 2 minutes
Total distance: 210 yards

RUNNING FORM –
CLOCK ENDURANCE RUNS (Contd...)

Set three

5 × A to 9:00, 9:00 to 3:00, 3:00 to 4:30, 4:30 to 6:00, 6:00 to 12:00, 12:00 to A

Work:rest ratio: 1:3 pre-season, 1:2 in season

Recovery between sets: 2 minutes

Total distance: 240 yards

Set four

6 × A to 10:30, 10:30 to 1:30, 1:30 to A, A to 7:30, 7:30 to 4:30, 4:30 to A, A to 12:00, 12:00 to A

Work:rest ratio: 1:3 pre-season, 1:2 in season

Recovery between sets: 2 minutes

Total distance: 360 yards

Total session distance: 930 yards

Variations/progressions

- Add codes for certain strokes to be performed at certain parts of the clock, i.e. 12:00 – lunge volley, 6:00 – backhand, etc.
- Start the run from different sections on the clock
- Vary the recovery time between sets
- Vary the work:rest ratio
- Introduce an active recovery between runs

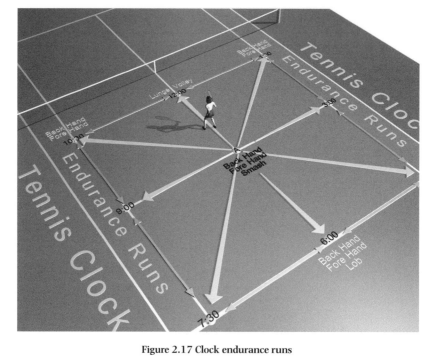

Figure 2.17 Clock endurance runs

DRILL | *ENDURANCE TRAINING –* *INTERVAL RUNNING SESSIONS*

Aim
To develop tennis-specific endurance.

Area/equipment
Indoor or outdoor area; marker dots set out at different distances as described in 'Sets and reps' below.

Description
Player runs at a medium to high intensity for the distances set out in 'Sets and reps' below. The work:rest ratio is to be calculated by the time taken to complete the run; for example in session E, set 1 (10 × 20 m), if a single run takes you 5 seconds then you would rest for 10 seconds before completing the second run, and so on. On completing the set of 10, you would take a 3-minute active recovery (walking) before moving on to the second set of 5 × 50 m.

These interval runs are fantastic for developing endurance; they have a major impact on a player's VO_2 max without the need for running long, slow miles, and they also maintain a player's ability to be explosive, as they maintain fast-twitch fibres instead of recruiting slow-twitch fibres. Ensure that you warm up with 10 minutes of Dynamic Flex. Try to organise your training schedule so that you have at least 48 hours recovery between intense interval sessions.

Sets and reps

SESSION A

3 × 200 m
4 × 100 m
5 × 50 m
10 × 25 m
10 × 10 m

Work:rest ratio: 1:3
Recovery between sets: 3 minutes
For the 25 m and 10 m runs, players should start from different standing positions e.g. backwards (turn to both sides) or sideways.

SESSION B

5 × 250 m
5 × 150 m
5 × 100 m

Work:rest ratio: 1:3. The recovery between reps should be active (i.e. walking).
Recovery between sets: 3 minutes between sets 1 and 2; 2 minutes between sets 2 and 3

ENDURANCE TRAINING –
INTERVAL RUNNING SESSIONS (Contd...)

SESSION C

10 × 75 m	Work:rest ratio: 1:3
10 × 50 m	Work:rest ratio: 1:3
10 × 30 m	Work:rest ratio: 1:2
10 × 20 m	Work:rest ratio: 1:2
20 × 5 m	Immediate turn around and repeat

Recovery between sets: 3 minutes

SESSION D

1 × 150 m
1 × 100 m
1 × 50 m
2 × 25 m
4 × 10 m
5 × 10 m

Work:rest ratio: 1:3
Players should complete session D five times with a full 3-minute recovery between each set.

SESSION E

10 × 20 m	Work:rest ratio: 1:2
5 × 50 m	Work:rest ratio: 1:3
6 × 25 m	Work:rest ratio: 1:2
3 × 100 m	Work:rest ratio: 1:3
4 × 75 m	Work:rest ratio: 1:3
10 × 15 m	Work:rest ratio: 1:1.5

Recovery between sets: 3 minutes

SESSION F

5 × 10 m	Work:rest ratio: 1:1.5
10 × 15 m	Work:rest ratio: 1:1.5
5 × 100 m	Work:rest ratio: 1:2.5
3 × 150 m	Work:rest ratio: 1:3
5 × 15 m	Work:rest ratio: 1:2
3 × 20 m	Work:rest ratio: 1:2

Recovery between sets: 3 minutes

ENDURANCE TRAINING –
INTERVAL RUNNING SESSIONS (Contd...)

SESSION G

5 × 80 m	Work:rest ratio: 1:2.5
5 × 25 m	Work:rest ratio: 1:2
5 × 50 m	Work:rest ratio: 1:2
5 × 60 m	Work:rest ratio: 1:3
5 × 30 m	Work:rest ratio: 1:2

Variations/progressions
- Use different starting positions
- Markers to be set out at different angles

DRILL

SPEED ENDURANCE –
INTERVAL RUNNING SESSIONS

Aim
To develop a player's ability to recover and repeat short explosive bursts of activities.

Area/equipment
Indoor or outdoor area; marker dots set out at different distances as described in 'Sets and reps' below.

Description
Player performs high-intensity runs as described in 'Sets and reps' below.

Sets and Reps

SESSION A

5 × 80 m
5 × 25 m
5 × 50 m
5 × 60 m
5 × 30 m

Work:rest ratio: 1:2
Recovery between sets: 3 minutes

SESSION B

6 × 40 m	Work:rest ratio: 1:2
6 × 50 m	Work:rest ratio: 1:2
6 × 30 m	Work:rest ratio: 1:2
6 × 20 m	Work:rest ratio: 1:2
20 × 5 m	Immediate turn around and repeat

Recovery between sets: 3 minutes

SESSION C

5 × 50 m	Work:rest ratio: 1:2
5 × 80 m	Forwards for 40 m, backwards for 10 m and then forwards for 30 m Work:rest ratio of 1:2.5
5 × 40 m	Work:rest ratio: 1:2
5 × 80 m	Forwards for 40 m, backwards for 10 m and then forwards for 30 m Work:rest ratio of 1:2.5
5 × 50 m	Work:rest ratio: 1:2

Recovery between sets: 3 minutes

SPEED ENDURANCE –
INTERVAL RUNNING SESSIONS (Contd...)

SESSION D

    6 × 40 m: forwards for 20 m, turn and run for 10 m, turn again
                 and run for 10 m
    8 × 20 m: to be completed from different starting positions
    6 × 40 m: as set 1
    8 × 20 m: as set 2
    6 × 30 m: forwards for 10 m, backwards for 10 m then forwards
                 for 10 m

Work:rest ratio: 1:2
Recovery between sets: 3 minutes
Sets 2 and 4 should be completed from different starting positions,
which you should select from the variations and progressions below.
Be sure to vary them within the set and from session to session.

Variations/progressions

Use the following starting positions:

- Forward split stance – be sure to alternate the leading leg
- Forward parallel stance – again, be sure to alternate the foot that
makes the first step
- Sideways stance – turn and go, bearing the above point in mind
- Backwards stance – turn and go, turning on alternate shoulders

CHAPTER 3 INNERVATION

FAST FEET, AGILITY, CO-ORDINATION, BALANCE AND CONTROL FOR TENNIS

Tennis places incredible demands on a player's ability to move quickly in all directions: to change direction, decelerate, stop instantly and start again, jump into the air, land and instantly move off in another direction, all the time maintaining balance and control to hit the ball with efficient and effective power. This complex sequence of movements can be practised and perfected during the innervation stage of the SAQ Continuum.

Innervation is the transition stage from warm-up and mechanics to periods of high-intensity work that activate the neural pathways. Using Fast Foot Ladders, dance-like patterns such as twists, jumps and turns are all introduced, increasing the rate of firing in the neuro-muscular system.

Once the basic footwork patterns have been mastered, more advanced, tennis-specific footwork drills that require speed, co-ordination, agility and dynamic balance can be introduced. The key here is to speed up the movement techniques without compromising the quality of the player's mechanics. The drills in this chapter progress from simple footwork patterns to complex tennis-specific drills that include split, jab, pivot, gravity, recovery and shuffle steps.

DRILL   *FAST FOOT LADDER – SINGLE RUN*

Aim
To develop linear fast feet with control, precision and power.

Area/equipment
Half a tennis court or an indoor or outdoor grid 13 yards in length. Tennis racket. Fast Foot Ladder (ensure that this is the correct ladder for the type of surface being used).

Description
Player covers the length of the ladder by placing a foot in each ladder space (see Fig. 3.1(a)). Return to the start by jogging back beside the ladder.

Key teaching points
- Maintain correct running form/mechanics
- Start slowly and gradually increase the speed
- Maintain an upright posture
- Stress that quality not quantity is important

Sets and reps
3 sets of 4 reps with a 1-minute recovery between each set.

Variations/progressions
- Single lateral step – as above but performed laterally (see Fig. 3.1(b))
- In and out – move sideways along the ladder stepping into and out of each ladder space, i.e. both feet in and both feet out (see Fig. 3.1(c))
- 'Icky Shuffle' – side-stepping movement into and out of each ladder space while moving forwards (see Fig. 3.1(d))
- Double run – perform as single run above, but with both feet in each ladder space (see Fig. 3.1(e))
- Hopscotch (see Fig. 3.1(f))
- Single-space jumps – two-footed jumps into and out of each ladder space (see Fig. 3.1(g))
- Two forwards and one back (see Fig. 3.1(h))
- 'Spotty Dogs' (see Fig. 3.1(i))
- 'Twist Again' (see Fig. 3.1(j))
- Hops in and out (see Fig. 3.1(k))
- Carioca (see Fig. 3.1(l))

FAST FOOT LADDER – SINGLE RUN (Contd...)

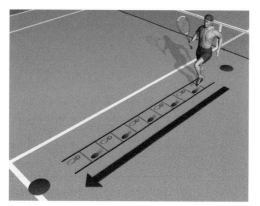

Figure 3.1(a) Fast Foot Ladder – single run

Figure 3.1(b) Fast Foot Ladder – single lateral step

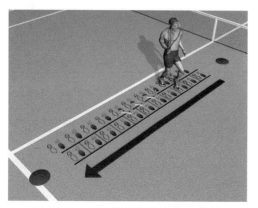

Figure 3.1(c) Fast Foot Ladder – in and out

Figure 3.1(d) Fast Foot Ladder – 'Icky Shuffle'

Figure 3.1(e) Fast Foot Ladder – double run

Figure 3.1(f) Fast Foot Ladder – hopscotch

FAST FOOT LADDER – SINGLE RUN (Contd...)

Figure 3.1(g) Fast Foot Ladder – single-space jumps

Figure 3.1(h) Fast Foot Ladder – two forwards and one back

Figure 3.1(i) Fast Foot Ladder – 'Spotty Dogs'

Figure 3.1(j) Fast Foot Ladder – 'Twist Again'

Figure 3.1(k) Fast Foot Ladder – hops in and out

Figure 3.1(l) Fast Foot Ladder – carioca

DRILL   FAST FOOT LADDER – JAB STEP

Aim
To develop a fast, controlled first forward step, with the lead foot in the direction of the on-coming ball.

Area/equipment
Half a tennis court or an indoor or outdoor area grid 13 yards in length. Tennis racket and tennis ball. 7.5-feet piece of outdoor/indoor Fast Foot Ladder. 4 different-coloured marker dots.

Description
Put the ladder on the ground and place a coloured marker dot in each of the ladder squares (in a 7.5-foot ladder there are 4 squares) – a blue marker in the far left box, a red marker centre-left, a yellow marker centre-right and a green marker far right. The player stands in a lateral position facing the ladder opposite the red and yellow marker dots. The drill commences with the player shuffling on the spot; the coach then randomly calls a colour and the player has to move his or her opposite foot across and jab the nominated coloured marker, then return immediately to the centre position ready for the next call. Therefore, the left foot will jab the green and yellow markers while the right foot will jab the red and blue markers. See Fig. 3.2.

Key teaching points
■ Maintain an athletic position
■ Maintain correct form/mechanics
■ Use short steps and work on the balls of the feet
■ Keep off the heels
■ Do not sink into the hips

Sets and reps
5 sets of 1 minute with a 1-minute recovery between sets.

Variation/progression
Coach to throw a tennis ball in front of the square nominated for the player to return.

Figure 3.2 Fast Foot Ladder – jab step

DRILL   FAST FOOT LADDER – T FORMATION

Aim
To develop speed of acceleration when chasing a ball or setting off on a run; to develop the transfer from linear to lateral running.

Area/equipment
Half a tennis court or an indoor or outdoor grid 13 yards in length. Tennis racket and tennis ball. Place 2 ladders in a T formation, with 1 marker dot at the start and a marker dot at each end of the head of the T.

Description
Player accelerates down the ladder using single steps. On reaching the head of the T, he/she transfers from linear steps to lateral steps. On coming out of the ladder, the player accelerates forwards for 2–3 yards and then decelerates. See Fig. 3.3(a).

Figure 3.3(a) Fast Foot Ladder – T formation

Key teaching points
- Maintain correct running form/mechanics
- Use a strong arm drive when transferring from linear to lateral steps
- Use short steps when turning; do not cross the feet

Sets and reps
3 sets of 4 reps (2 moving to the left and 2 to the right) with a 1-minute recovery between each set.

Variations/progressions
- Start with a lateral run and, upon reaching the end ladder, accelerate in a straight line forwards down the ladder. On reaching the end, turn and accelerate back towards the starting line
- Coach stands 6–7 yards away from the head of the T and, while the player is moving laterally through the ladder, delivers a ball for the player to move on to and return (see Fig. 3.3(b))
- Mix and match the Fast Foot Ladder drills described earlier (see pages 79–81)

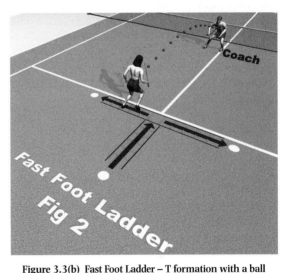

Figure 3.3(b) Fast Foot Ladder – T formation with a ball

DRILL FAST FOOT LADDER – CROSSOVER

Aim
To develop speed, agility and change of direction in a more pressured and crowded area; to improve reaction time, peripheral vision, timing and concentration.

Area/equipment
Half a tennis court or an indoor or outdoor grid 13 yards in length. Tennis racket and tennis ball. Place 4 ladders in a cross formation, leaving a clear centre square of about 3 square yards. Place a marker dot 1 yard from the start of each ladder.

Description
Place one player at the start of each ladder. Simultaneously, they accelerate down the ladder performing a single-step drill; on reaching the end of the ladder, they accelerate across the centre square and join the end of the queue. They do not travel down this ladder. See Fig. 3.4(a).

Key teaching points
- Maintain correct running form/mechanics
- Keep the head and eyes up and be aware of other players, particularly around the centre area

Sets and reps
3 sets of 6 reps with a 1-minute recovery between each set.

Variations/progressions
- At the end of the first ladder, side-step to the right or left and join the end of the appropriate adjacent ladder (see Fig. 3.4(b))
- Vary the Fast Foot Ladder drills performed down the first ladder
- Include a 360-degree turn in the centre square; this is effective for developing body and positional awareness

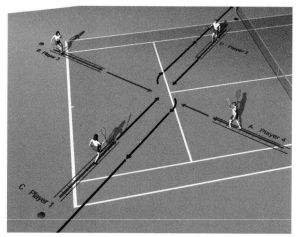

Figure 3.4(a) Fast Foot Ladder – crossover

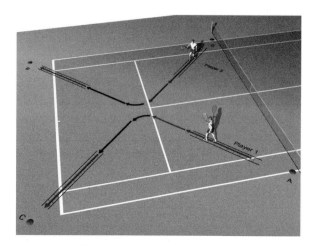

Figure 3.4(b) Fast Foot Ladder – crossover with side-step

DRILL FAST FOOT LADDER – MIRROR STEPS

Aim
To develop explosive footwork patterns; to improve reactions and responses to complex movement situations.

Area/equipment
Half a tennis court or an indoor or outdoor area. Tennis racket and tennis ball. 15-foot section of Fast Foot Ladder.

Description
Players 1 and 2 stand opposite each other on either side of the ladder. Starting in the middle, player 1 moves laterally and randomly steps in and out of the ladder. Player 2 responds by mirroring as quickly and as accurately as possible the movements of player 1. See Fig. 3.5.

Key teaching points
■ Maintain correct lateral running form/mechanics
■ Use short, sharp, explosive steps
■ Work off the balls of the feet
■ Use a strong arm drive
■ Always keep the hips square

Sets and reps
3 sets of 2 reps with a 15-second recovery between reps and a 2-minute recovery between each set. NB: In each set, each player should take the lead for 45 seconds.

Variations/progressions
■ Tennis ball to be passed between players at regular intervals to stimulate reactions
■ Players to simulate tennis strokes; these should also be mirrored
■ Use two 15-foot ladders, 3–4 yards apart. Players should mirror each other while moving in the separate ladders. The distance between them can be used for bouncing or hitting balls to each other at the same time

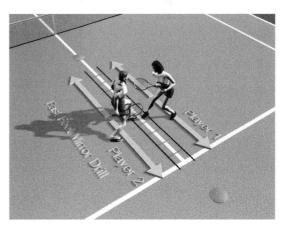

Figure 3.5 Fast Foot Ladder – mirror steps

DRILL　FAST FOOT LADDER – MOVE AND RETURN

Aim
To develop fast feet, dynamic balance, co-ordination, speed and agility while moving into position to strike a tennis ball.

Area/equipment
Half a tennis court or an indoor or outdoor area. Tennis racket and tennis ball. Place a 7.5-foot Fast Foot Ladder on the ground with a marker dot about 1 yard away from each end.

Description
Player 1 performs fast foot drills down the ladder either laterally or linearly; player 2, standing 2 yards away from the ladder in a central position, throws or hits the ball at different heights and angles, requiring player 1 to return the ball from different positions and under different pressures. See Fig. 3.6.

Key teaching points
- Concentrate on good footwork patterns
- Ensure that correct technical skills are used when shots are played
- Ensure that the player performing the drill reverts to correct running form/mechanics after returning the ball

Sets and reps
3 sets of 6 reps with a 1-minute recovery between each set.

Variations/progressions
- Vary the Fast Foot Ladder drills performed by player 1
- Use a 15-foot Fast Foot Ladder

Figure 3.6 Fast Foot Ladder – move and return

DRILL   *FAST FOOT LADDER – GIANT CROSSOVER*

Aim
To develop fast feet, speed, agility, dynamic balance, co-ordination, peripheral vision and reaction time when playing shots.

Area/equipment
Full tennis court or a large indoor or outdoor area. Tennis rackets, 2 or 4 tennis balls. Place 4 ladders in a cross formation with 25 yards between them in the centre area.

Description
Split the group into 4 equal groups and locate 1 group at the start of each ladder. The first player from each group accelerates down his/her ladder, performing fast foot drills. On entering the centre space, 2 players will hit the ball across the space for the oncoming player to return to the next oncoming player; this now becomes a continuous process. Having finished the shot, the player now joins the queue on the opposite side of the cross without travelling down the opposite ladder.

Key teaching points
- This should be a continuous drill
- Maintain correct running form/mechanics
- Correct technical skills must be used when players are on the ball
- Players should use clear communication

Sets and reps
3 sets of 6 reps with a 1-minute recovery between each set.

Variation/progression
Instead of using rackets, get the players to throw the ball to each other at different heights.

DRILL
FAST FOOT LADDER –
4-CORNER COURT COMBINATION

Aim
To develop acceleration, dynamic balance, control, reaction and peripheral vision while working with other players.

Area/equipment
Whole tennis court, 4 × 15-foot Fast Foot Ladders, rackets and balls. Place ladders at each corner of the court, 1 yard in from the singles line with first rung starting on the base line. Label the ladders A, B, C and D. Divide the players into 4 groups and line one group behind each ladder.

Description
The drill commences with player 1 accelerating down ladder A. He/she hits a ball to player 4, who has accelerated down ladder D. Player 1 then returns to the back of the group at ladder A; player 4 hits the ball to the next player accelerating down ladder A, then returns to the back of the group at ladder D. The drill becomes continuous, with the ball being hit between the two groups in the centre of the grid as they come out of the ladders. The drill is performed simultaneously between the groups at ladders B and C. See Fig. 3.7.

Key teaching points
- Maintain good form/mechanics
- Keep the head and eyes up
- Use a drop step when turning to get back to the start of the ladder
- Use correct tennis techniques

Sets and reps
3 sets of 2 minutes with a 1-minute recovery between each set.

Variation/progression
Players on ladder A return to the start of ladder B after completing the shot; players on ladder B return to the start of ladder A after completing the shot; the same applies to the players on ladders C and D. Therefore, the players will cross over between the two ladders on their side of the court.

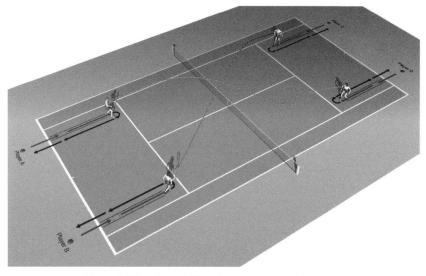

Figure 3.7 Fast Foot Ladder – 4-corner court combination

DRILL FAST FEET – LINE DRILLS

Aim
To develop quickness of the feet.

Area/equipment
Half a tennis court or an indoor or outdoor area. Tennis racket and tennis ball. Use any line marked on the ground.

Description
Players perform single split steps over the line and back. See Fig. 3.8(a).

Figure 3.8(a) Single split steps

Key teaching points
- Maintain good arm mechanics
- Maintain an upright posture
- Maintain a strong core
- Try to develop a rhythm
- Keep the head and eyes up

Sets and reps
3 sets of 20 reps with a 1-minute recovery between each set.

Variations/progressions
- Two-footed jumps over the line and back (see Fig. 3.8(b))
- Stand astride the line and bring the feet in to touch the line before moving them out again. Perform the drill as quickly as possible (see Fig. 3.8(c))
- Two-footed side jumps over the line and back (see Fig. 3.8(d))
- Two-footed side jumps with a 180-degree twist in the air over the line and back (see Fig. 3.8(e))
- Single quick hops
- Complex variation – introduce the ball either at the end of the drill for the player to explode on to and return, or during the drill for the player to return before continuing

Figure 3.8(b) Two-footed jumps

FAST FEET – LINE DRILLS (Contd...)

Figure 3.8(c) Astride the line

Figure 3.8(d) Two-footed side jumps

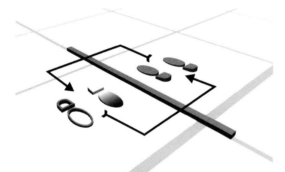

Figure 3.8(e) Two-footed side jumps with a 180-degree twist

DRILL   QUICK BOX STEPS AND JUMPS

Aim
To develop explosive power and control. NB: The emphasis is on speed.

Area/equipment
Half a tennis court or an indoor or outdoor area. Tennis racket and tennis ball. Bench, aerobics step or suitable strong box with a non-slip surface, about 12 inches high.

Description
Player performs an alternated split step on the box, i.e. one foot on the box and one on the floor. See Fig. 3.9(a).

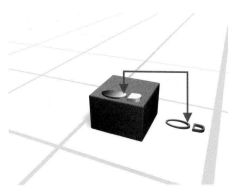

Figure 3.9(a) Alternated split step

Key teaching points
- Focus on a good arm drive
- Maintain an upright posture
- Maintain a strong core
- Keep the head and eyes up
- Work off the balls of the feet
- Work at a high intensity
- Try to develop a rhythm

Sets and reps
3 sets of 20 reps with a 1-minute recovery between each set.

Variations/progressions
- Two-footed jumps on and off the box (see Fig. 3.9(b))
- Two-footed side jumps on and off the box (see Fig. 3.9(c))
- Straddle jumps (see Fig. 3.9(d))
- Single-footed hops on and off the box (10 reps leading with the left foot and 10 leading with the right) (see Fig. 3.9(e))
- Alternate single hops – single hop onto the box to land on the opposite foot. Take off to land on the other side of the box, again on the opposite foot (see Fig. 3.9(f))

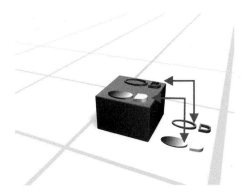

Figure 3.9(b) Two-footed jump

QUICK BOX STEPS AND JUMPS (Contd...)

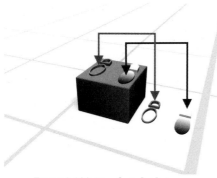

Figure 3.9(c) Two-footed side jump

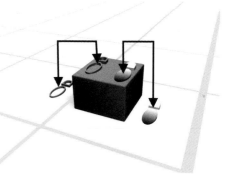

Figure 3.9(d) Straddle jump

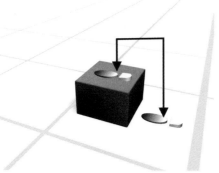

Figure 3.9(e) Single-footed hop

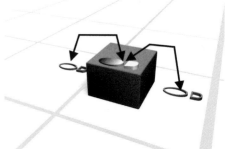

Figure 3.9(f) Alternate single hop

DRILL *FAST FEET –*
EYE–HAND CO-ORDINATION DEVELOPMENT

Aim
To develop lightning-fast feet and eye–hand co-ordination.

Area/equipment
Half a tennis court or an indoor or outdoor area. Tennis racket, Sidestrike, tennis ball.

Description
Player performs lateral footwork patterns on the Sidestrike (see Fig. 3.10). When the drill has been perfected, the ball is introduced for the player to return.

Key teaching points
- Work off the balls of the feet
- Maintain a strong core
- Keep the hips square
- Develop a rhythm
- Use correct catching and throwing techniques

Sets and reps
5 sets of 30 seconds with a 45-second recovery between sets and a 3-minute recovery after all sets have been completed. NB: this is a very high-intensity drill.

Variations/progressions
- Perform jab steps
- Perform cross-over steps
- Introduce the ball for the player to catch and return
- Work with a partner who stands 5 yards in front of the Sidestrike and randomly drops the ball for the player to explode on to

Figure 3.10 Fast feet – eye–hand co-ordination development

CHAPTER 4 ACCUMULATION OF POTENTIAL

THE SAQ TENNIS CIRCUIT

This is the part of the SAQ Continuum that brings together the areas of work already practised. Many of the mechanics and fast feet drills develop a specific skill; however, in tennis the different skills are rarely isolated but occur in quick succession or in combinations. An example of this is when a player, after serving from the base line, runs at full speed to the net to cut off angles and force the opponent into a particular shot. The opponent may now lob the ball, causing the player to turn explosively and accelerate back down the court to get into position to attempt to return the ball. Combinations of manoeuvres occur over different timespans throughout a game of tennis. Research has confirmed that phases of play during a tennis match usually last for 3–10 seconds on clay courts and 2–5 seconds on grass courts (Roetert et al., 2003), which also indicates that the movements being used are short and very explosive. Using ladders, hurdles, marker dots, poles, rackets, tennis balls and so on, tennis-specific circuits can be used to develop programmed agility and condition the player for this type of high-intensity multi-directional work.

The SAQ Tennis Circuit is also an excellent time for the coach and trainer to assess the quality of movement being used. If at any time within the circuit technique deteriorates, more time needs to be spent on the mechanics and innervation stages.

This phase should not fatigue players. Plan for high-intensity, high-quality movement rather than the quantity of sets and reps, and ensure a maximum recovery period between sets and reps.

DRILL AGILITY RUNS – 4-CORNER BALL

Aim
To develop multi-directional explosive agility, turn mechanics and running mechanics.

Area/equipment
Indoor or outdoor area of about 10 square yards. Tennis racket. Place 1 marker on each corner and 1 in the middle of the square.

Description
Player starts at the centre marker E, then accelerates out to and around marker A and back to marker E. The player then completes the drill by going out and around markers B, C and D (this is 1 repetition). See Fig. 4.1.

Key teaching points
- Maintain correct running form/mechanics
- Use strong arm mechanics, both with and without the ball
- Keep tight to the markers on the turns
- Work off the balls of the feet

Sets and reps
3 sets of 2 reps with a 1-minute recovery between reps and a 2-minute recovery between sets.

Variations/progressions
- Player runs through the circuit while controlling the ball with the racket
- Place a tennis ball on each outer marker A, B, C and D. Player sprints to the marker, scoops up the ball and returns it to marker E. This is continued for all four balls

Figure 4.1 Agility runs – 4-corner ball

DRILL   ZIGZAG RUNS

Aim
To develop fast, co-ordinated and controlled angled lateral runs.

Area/equipment
Half a tennis court or an indoor or outdoor area. Tennis racket and tennis ball. Mark out a grid using 10–12 markers or poles in 2 lines of 5–6. Stagger them so that the line is a zigzag formation. See Fig. 4.2(a).

Description
Player runs the zigzag formation, staying on the inside of the markers, then walks back to the start before repeating the drill.

Key teaching points
- Maintain correct running form/mechanics
- Players must keep their hips facing in the direction in which they are running
- Use short steps
- Do not skip
- Use good arm mechanics (arm mechanics are as vital in lateral movements as they are in linear movements; many players forget to use their arms when they are moving sideways)

Sets and reps
3 sets of 6 reps with a walk-back recovery between each rep and a 1-minute recovery between each set.

Variations/progressions
- Perform the drill backwards
- Player goes around the outside of each marker rather than staying on the inside of them
- Up-and-back – enter the grid sideways and move forwards to the first marker, backwards to the next and so on
- Add a Fast Foot Ladder to the start and finish for acceleration and deceleration running (see Fig. 4.2(b))

Figure 4.2(a) Zigzag run

Figure 4.2(b) Zigzag run with Fast Foot Ladder

DRILL   *MOVEMENT CIRCUIT*

Aim
To develop the running patterns likely to be encountered in a game of tennis.

Area/equipment
Half a tennis court or an indoor or outdoor area. Tennis racket and tennis ball. Markers, hurdles, Fast Foot Ladders and poles, placed in a circuit within the area (see Fig. 4.3(a)).

Description
Player follows the circuit, which will take them through ladders, stepping and jumping over hurdles, side-stepping through markers, running backwards, jumping and turning. NB: one circuit should take the players 30–60 seconds to complete.

Key teaching point
Maintain correct running form/mechanics for all activities.

Sets and Reps
1 set of 6 reps with a varied recovery time between each rep, depending on the stage of the season:
- early pre-season: work:recovery ratio of 1:3
- middle to late pre-season: work:recovery ratio of 1:2
- late pre-season and in-season: work:recovery ratio of 1:1

Variations/progressions
- At certain points within the circuit introduce a tennis ball to be hit using different types of shots
- Vary the circuit and the drills on a regular basis, using imagination and tennis knowledge (see Fig. 4.3(b) for an example)

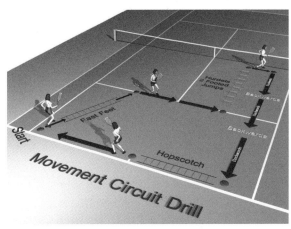

Figure 4.3(a) Movement circuit

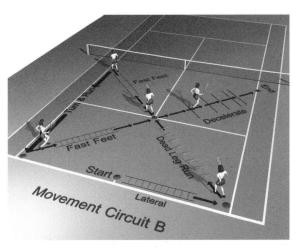

Figure 4.3(b) Movement circuit – variation

CHAPTER 5 EXPLOSION

THREE-STEP, MULTI-DIRECTIONAL ACCELERATION FOR TENNIS

The exercises outlined in this chapter have been designed to boost response times and develop multi-directional, explosive movements.

Programmable and random agility are trained using resisted and assisted high-quality plyometrics. Plyometrics exercises focus on the stretch–shortening cycle of the muscles involved, an action that is a central part of tennis performance. Plyometrics drills include drop-jumps, hops, skips and bounds. Plyometrics can be fun and challenging and adds variety to training sessions; however, there is potential for injury with these exercises so they must be performed using the correct technique and at the correct point in the training session.

Upper-body speed and power are also catered for with jelly-ball workouts, which develop the kind of strength required for making shots. These workouts also develop the power used for arm drives, which can dramatically improve running speed and jumping height.

The crucial element of explosive drills is the implementation of the 'contrast' phase. This simply means performing the drill without resistance for one or two reps immediately after performing it with resistance. The non-resisted movements will naturally be more explosive and more easily remembered and reproduced over a period of time.

The key here is to ensure that quality, not quantity is the priority. Efforts must be carefully monitored – this is a time for high-intensity explosive action, not 'tongue-hanging-out' fatigue!

DRILL SEATED FORWARD GET-UPS

Aim
To develop multi-directional explosive acceleration; to improve a player's ability to get up and accelerate all in one movement.

Area/equipment
Half a tennis court or an indoor or outdoor area of about 20 square yards. Tennis racket and tennis ball.

Description
Player sits on the floor, facing in the direction she/he is going to run with legs straight out in front. On the coach's signal, the player gets up as quickly as possible, accelerates for 10 yards and then slows down before jogging gently back to the start position.

Key teaching points
- Try to complete the drill in one smooth action
- Use correct running form/mechanics
- Do not stop between getting up and starting to run
- Get into an upright position and drive the arms as soon as possible
- Ensure the initial steps are short and powerful
- Do not over-stride

Sets and reps
3 sets of 5 reps with a jog-back recovery between each rep and a 2-minute recovery between each set.

Variations/progressions
- Seated backward get-ups
- Seated sideways get-ups
- Lying get-ups from the front, back, left and right
- Kneeling get-ups
- Work in pairs and have get-up competitions, with players chasing a ball
- Work in pairs with one player in front of the other; perform 'tag' get-ups

DRILL LET-GOES

Aim
To develop multi-directional explosive acceleration.

Area/equipment
Indoor or outdoor area of 20 square yards; Viper Belt with hand leash.

Description
Player 1 wears the Viper Belt and attempts to accelerate away in a straight line forwards while being resisted from behind by player 2, who holds the hand leash to provide resistance. Player 2 maintains the resistance for a couple of seconds by shuffling and holding player 1 as they slowly go forwards before releasing player 1, who explodes away. (If a Viper Belt and hand leash are not available, hold on to the shirt/top of player 1.)

Key teaching points
- Player 1 should not lean or pull forwards excessively
- Use short steps during the explosion and acceleration phases
- Use a good arm drive
- Player 1 should adopt good running form/mechanics as soon as possible after being released

Sets and reps
3 sets of 5 reps with a walk-back recovery between each rep and a 2-minute recovery between each set.

Variations/progressions
- Lateral let-goes
- Backward let-goes
- Various angled let-goes
- Let-goes with an acceleration onto a drop ball, with the ball to be hit before the second bounce

DRILL   *CHAIR GET-UPS*

Aim
To develop explosive power for acceleration, linearly and laterally.

Area/equipment
Half a tennis court or an indoor or outdoor area with plenty of room for deceleration. Tennis racket. Place a chair/stool and 5 markers as shown in Fig. 5.1.

Description
Player sits on a chair and, on the coach's signal, gets up and moves to the nominated marker as quickly as possible. On reaching the marker the player should decelerate and walk back to the start position.

Key teaching points
- Use an explosive arm drive when getting up
- Get into a correct running posture as quickly as possible
- Initial steps should be short and powerful
- Work off the balls of the feet

Sets and reps
3 sets of 10 reps with a walk-back recovery between each rep and a 2-minute recovery between each set.

Variation/progression
Work in pairs; player 1 stands 1 or 2 yards away from the chair with 2 tennis balls and performs 'ball drops' by holding both arms out and dropping one of the balls for player 2 (seated) to either catch or hit with a racket.

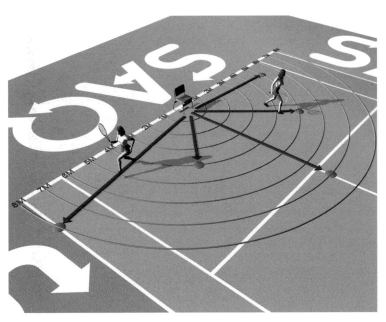

Figure 5.1 Chair get-ups

DRILL   *FLEXI-CORD – BUGGY RUNS*

Aim
To develop multi-directional explosive acceleration.

Area/equipment
Half a tennis court or an indoor or outdoor area with plenty of room for safe deceleration. Tennis racket. Viper Belt with a Flexi-cord attached at both ends by 2 anchor points. Place 3 markers in a line, 10 yards apart.

Description
Work in pairs. Player 1 wears the belt while Player 2 stands behind holding the Flexi-cord, hands looped in and over the cord for safety purposes. Player 2 allows resistance to develop as Player 1 accelerates forwards, then runs behind maintaining constant resistance over the first 10 yards. Both players need to decelerate over the second 10 yards. Player 1 removes the belt after the required number of reps and completes a solo contrast run. Then swap roles and repeat the drill.

Key teaching points
- Player 1 must focus on correct running form/mechanics and explosive drive
- Player 2 works with Player 1, allowing the Flexi-cord to provide the resistance
- Always perform the drill once without resistance immediately afterwards (contrast phase)

Sets and reps
1 set of 6 reps plus 1 contrast run with a 30-second recovery between each rep and a 3-minute recovery before the next exercise.

Variations/progressions
- Lateral buggy run – Player 1 accelerates laterally for the first 2 yards before turning to cover the remaining distance linearly
- Player 2 to throw tennis ball over player 1's head; player 1 reacts and accelerates under resistance to hit the ball

DRILL FLEXI-CORD – OUT AND BACK

Aim
To develop short, explosive, angled accelerated runs.

Area/equipment
Half a tennis court or an indoor or outdoor area of 10 square yards. Tennis racket. Viper Belt with a Flexi-cord attached to 1 anchor point on the belt and a safety belt on the other end of the Flexi-cord. Marker dots set out as in Fig. 5.2.

Description
Work in pairs. Player 1 wears the Viper Belt; Player 2 stands directly behind player 1 holding the Flexi-cord and wearing the safety belt. The Flexi-cord should be taut at this stage. Player 2 nominates a marker for player 1, varying between the 3 markers for the required number of repetitions. Player 1 runs to the nominated marker, then returns to the start using short, sharp steps. Finish with a contrast run before swapping roles.

Key teaching points
- Focus on short, sharp explosive steps and a fast, powerful arm drive
- Maintain correct running form/mechanics
- Work off the balls of the feet
- Use short steps while returning to the start, and keep the weight forwards

Sets and reps
3 sets of 6 reps plus 1 contrast run per set with a 3-minute recovery between each set. For advanced players, depending on the time of the season, increase to 10 reps per set.

Variations/progressions
- Perform the drill laterally
- Work backwards using short, sharp steps
- A third player or coach serves a ball to player 1 to return as he/she reaches the designated marker

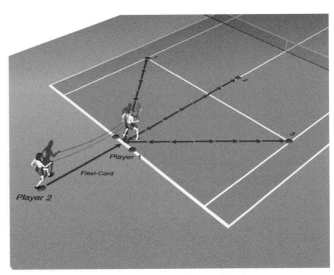

Figure 5.2 Flexi-cord out and back

DRILL

FLEXI-CORD – LATERAL
EXPLOSIVE FIRST STEP DEVELOPMENT

Aim
To develop explosive lateral movement ability, particularly over the first few yards.

Area/equipment
Half a tennis court or an indoor or outdoor area 12 yards square. Tennis racket. Viper Belt or Viper Swivel Belt, Flexi-cords, tennis balls and 13 markers set up as shown in Fig. 5.3.

Description
Player 1, wearing the Viper Belt, runs in a zigzag pattern between the markers. Player 2 works along the line between the 2 outside markers, slightly behind the partner to ensure that the Flexi-cord does not get in the way of the arm mechanics. Work up and back along the line of markers. On completing the reps, player 1 removes the belt and performs 1 contrast run.

Key teaching points
- Maintain correct running form/mechanics
- Use good technique for hitting the ball
- Use short steps going backwards
- Keep the hips square
- Player 2 to move along with player 1, concentrating on maintaining a constant distance, angle and resistance

Sets and reps
3 sets of 8 reps plus 2 contrast runs with a 3-minute recovery between each set.

Variations/progressions
- Introduce a third player or coach who throws the ball to player 1 during the drill
- Perform the drill linearly

Figure 5.3 Flexi-cord – lateral explosive first step development

DRILL RESISTED HIGH BACKHAND

Aim
To increase shoulder power and muscular endurance.

Area/equipment
Half a tennis court or an indoor or outdoor area 12 yards in length.
Punch/kick resistor.

Description
Player holds punch/kick resistor at both ends and performs a high
backhand range of movement while under resistance.

Key teaching points
- Maintain correct posture
- Use correct plane of motion required by the shot

Sets and reps
3 sets of 15 reps with a 1-minute recovery between sets.

Variation/progression
Player to perform the drill using a light handweight.

DRILL RESISTED SERVING POSITION

Aim
To increase elbow and shoulder power and muscular endurance.

Area/equipment
Half a tennis court or an indoor or outdoor area 13 yards in length.
Punch/kick resistor.

Description
Player holds punch/kick resistor at one end in his/her dominant hand.
The other end is placed on the floor and the player stands on it using
the foot on the same side of the body (i.e. if the player is right-handed,
he/she holds one end of the punch/kick resistor in the right hand and
stands on the other end with the right foot). The player then performs
a serve range of movement while under resistance.

Key teaching points
■ Maintain correct posture
■ Use the correct plane of motion required by the shot
■ Use the other hand to support the elbow of the dominant arm

Sets and reps
3 sets of 15 reps with a 1-minute recovery between sets.

Variation/progression
Player to perform the drill using a light handweight.

DRILL   *FLEXI-CORD – OVERSPEED*

Aim
To develop lightning-quick acceleration.

Area/equipment
Half a tennis court or an indoor or outdoor area 13 yards in length. Tennis racket. 8 marker dots and 1 Viper Belt with a Flexi-cord. Markers placed to show starting point, partner position and different angles to accelerate on to. See Fig. 5.4.

Description
Work in pairs. Player 1 wears the Viper Belt and faces player 2, who holds the Flexi-cord and has the safety belt around his/her waist, i.e. the Flexi-cord will go from belly button to belly button. Player 1 stands at marker A, player 2 stands at marker B and walks backwards away from player 1, thereby increasing the cord's resistance. After the cord has been stretched for 4–5 yards, player 1 accelerates towards player 2, who then nominates marker C or D, requiring player 1 to change direction explosively. Walk back to the start and repeat the drill.

Key teaching points
- Maintain correct running form/mechanics
- Control the running form/mechanics
- During the change of direction phase, shorten the steps and increase the firing rate of the arms

Sets and reps
3 sets of 8 reps plus 1 contrast run with a 3-minute recovery between each set.

Variations/progressions
- Player 1 starts with a horizontal jump before accelerating away
- Introduce a ball for player 1 to return from different angles during the acceleration

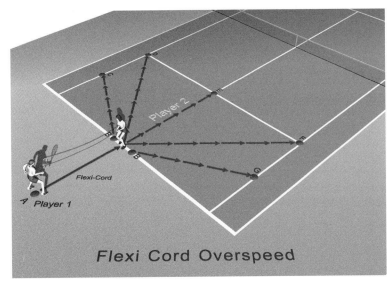

Figure 5.4 Flexi-cord – overspeed

DRILL   SIDE-STEPPER – RESISTED LATERAL RUNS

Aim
To develop explosive, controlled lateral patterns of running and movement.

Area/equipment
Half a tennis court or an indoor or outdoor area. Tennis racket, Side-Stepper. Place 10–12 marker dots in a zigzag pattern.

Description
The player wearing the Side-Stepper runs in a lateral zigzag between the markers down the length of the grid and, just before a marker, extends the last step to increase the level of resistance, then turns round and works back along the grid. See Fig. 5.5.

Key teaching points
■ Maintain correct lateral running form/mechanics
■ Do not sink into the hips when stepping off to change direction
■ During the change of direction phase, increase arm speed to provide additional control

Sets and reps
3 sets of 6 reps plus 1 contrast run with a 3-minute recovery between each set.

Variations/progressions
■ Perform the drill backwards
■ Introduce a tennis ball at the point where the player is changing direction for him/her to play a shot

Side Stepper Resisted Lateral Run

Figure 5.5 Side-Stepper – resisted lateral runs

DRILL

SIDE-STEPPER – LATERAL SIDE, SHUFFLE AND CROSS-OVER STEPS

Aim

To develop explosive lateral/angled side-steps, shuffle and cross-over steps.

Area/equipment

Half a tennis court or an indoor or outdoor area. Tennis racket, tennis balls, Side-Stepper. Place 4 marker dots to form a rectangle measuring 2.5 × 5 yards.

Description

Two players stand facing each other, one at each end of the grid between the marker dots that are 2.5 yards apart. One player is wearing the Side-Stepper and the other player is holding the tennis balls. The player with the tennis balls serves the ball so that the player wearing the Side-Stepper has to move laterally to return it. This drill is then repeated for the required amount of time. The player serving the ball should ensure that the ball is delivered at different angles and at different speeds. See Fig. 5.6.

Key teaching points

■ Use quick, low steps, *not* high knees
■ Do not skip or jump – one foot should be in contact with the floor at all times
■ Try to keep the feet shoulder-width apart
■ Use a powerful arm drive
■ Do not sink into the hips

Sets and reps

4 sets of 30-second reps, with a 30-second recovery between each set. Players should swap roles after the completion of the sets.

Variations/progressions

■ Player to perform shuffle steps while moving sideways
■ Player to perform cross-over steps while moving sideways
■ Both players to wear Side-Steppers and hit the ball to each other

Figure 5.6 Side-Stepper – lateral side, shuffle and cross-over steps

DRILL HANDWEIGHT DROPS

Aim
To develop explosive power, re-acceleration and, specifically, a powerful arm drive.

Area/equipment
Half a tennis court or an indoor or outdoor area. Tennis racket, tennis balls, handweights (2–4 lb). Position 1 marker dot to mark the start, a second 15 yards away and a final marker 10 yards away from the second.

Description
Player holds the weights in his/her hands and accelerates to the second marker where he/she releases the handweights, keeping a natural flow to the arm mechanics, then continues to accelerate to the third marker before decelerating and walking back to the start. Repeat the drill for the required number of reps.

Key teaching points
- Maintain correct running form/mechanics
- Do not stop the arm drive to release the weights
- Keep the head tall
- Quality not quantity is vital

Sets and reps
3 sets of 4 reps with a 3-minute recovery between each set.

Variations/progressions
- On the release of the handweights the coach can call a change of direction so that the player has to accelerate off at different angles
- Perform the drill backwards over the first 15 yards then turn, accelerate and release the weights to explode away
- Perform the drill laterally over the first 15 yards then turn, accelerate and release the weights to explode away
- On the release of the handweights the ball is thrown for the player to accelerate on to and catch

DRILL PARACHUTE RUNNING

Aim
To develop explosive running over longer distances (sprint endurance); to develop explosive re-acceleration.

Area/equipment
Indoor or outdoor area, 4 markers and a parachute. Mark out a grid 50 yards in length; place 1 marker dot for the start point and 3 further marker dots at distances of 30, 40 and 50 yards from the start marker.

Description
Wearing the parachute, the player accelerates to the 40-yard marker then decelerates to the end of the grid.

Key teaching points
- Maintain correct running form/mechanics
- Do not worry if the wind and the resistance make it feel as though you are being pulled from side to side; this will in fact improve your balance and co-ordination
- Do not lean into the run too much
- Quality not quantity is vital

Sets and reps
3 sets of 5 reps plus 1 contrast run with a walk-back recovery between each rep and a 3-minute recovery between each set.

Variations/progressions
- Explosive re-acceleration using the parachute's release mechanism – the player accelerates to the 30-yard marker where he/she releases the parachute, then explodes to the 40-yard marker before decelerating
- Random change of direction – the coach stands behind the 30-yard marker and, as the player releases the parachute, the coach indicates a change in the direction of the run. When mastered, the coach can then introduce the ball for players to run on to during the explosive phase

DRILL BALL DROPS

Aim
To develop explosive reactions.

Area/equipment
Half a tennis court or an indoor or outdoor area. Tennis racket, tennis balls.

Description
Working in pairs, player 1 drops the ball at various distances and angles from his/her partner. The ball is dropped from shoulder height and player 2 attempts to hit the ball before the second bounce. NB: Distances between players will differ because the height of the bounce will vary depending on the ground surface and make of ball.

Key teaching points
- Work off the balls of the feet, particularly before the drop
- Use a very explosive arm drive
- The initial steps should be short, fast and explosive
- At the take-off do not jump, dither or hesitate
- Work on developing a smooth one-movement run

Sets and reps
3 sets of 10 reps with a 2-minute recovery between each set.

Variations/progressions
- Player to hold 2 balls and to drop just 1
- Work in groups of 3 with 2 of the players at different angles alternately dropping a ball for the third player to hit; on doing so, the player turns and accelerates away to hit the second ball (see Fig. 5.7)
- Alter the start positions, e.g. sideways, backwards with a call, seated, etc.
- Use different balls, i.e. plastic, soft foam, hard rubber, to vary the bounce
- Players to stand closer together; player with the racket to volley the ball

Figure 5.7 Ball drops

DRILL   BREAK-AWAY MIRROR

Aim
To develop multi-directional explosive reactions.

Area/equipment
Half a tennis court or an indoor or outdoor area. Tennis racket, Break-Away Belt.

Description
Working in pairs, 2 players face each other attached by the Break-Away Belt. Set a time limit. Player 1 is the proactive player while player 2 is reactive. Player 1 attempts to get away from player 2 by using sideways, forward or backward movements. Players are not allowed to turn around and run away. The drill ends if and when the proactive player breaks the belt connection or the time runs out.

Key teaching points
- Stay focused on your partner
- Do not sink into the hips
- Keep the head tall and the spine straight
- Maintain correct arm mechanics

Sets and reps
3 sets where 1 set = 30 seconds of each player taking the proactive role followed by a 1-minute recovery period.

Variation/progression
Side-by-side mirror drills – the object is for the proactive player to move away laterally and gain as much distance as possible before the other can react.

DRILL   *W DRILL*

Aim
To develop explosive angled forward and backward movements.

Area/equipment
Half a tennis court or an indoor or outdoor area. Tennis racket, Viper Belt. Place 5 marker dots in a W formation, 6 yards wide at the top and 2 yards wide at the bottom, 4 yards to its longest point and 2 yards to the centre point.

Description
Wearing the Viper Belt, player 1 starts at point A of the W, moving under resistance backwards to point B, forwards to centre point C, backwards to point D and forwards to point E, which is 1 complete W. Player 2 works from behind and moves laterally to provide resistance as player 1 moves across the W. See Fig. 5.8.

Key teaching points
■ Focus on short, sharp, explosive steps
■ Use a powerful arm drive
■ Stay as tall as possible
■ Do not sink into the hips
■ Maintain correct running form at all times
■ Stay on the balls of the feet at all times
■ Use short steps in resisted backward movements

Sets and reps
3 sets of 5 reps where 1 rep = 1 complete W with a 2-minute recovery between each set.

Variations/progressions
■ Perform the drill laterally
■ Introduce a third player who stands in front and serves the ball for player 1 to return while performing the W drill

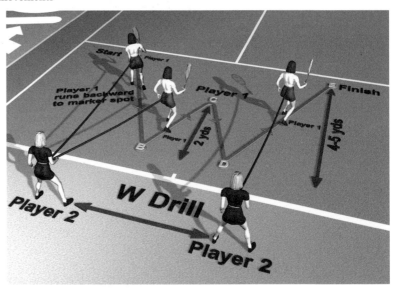

Figure 5.8 W drill

DRILL   *SLED RUNNING*

Aim
To develop explosive sprint endurance.

Area/equipment
Half a tennis court or an indoor or outdoor area. Tennis racket, marker dots and sprint sled. Mark out an area 30 yards long.

Description
The player is connected to the sled and sprints over the nominated distance before recovering, turning around and repeating the drill. See Fig. 5.9.

Key teaching points
- Maintain correct running form/mechanics
- Maintain a strong arm drive
- Often players will need to use an exaggerated forward lean to initiate the momentum required to get the sled moving
- As momentum picks up, the player should transfer to the correct running position

Sets and reps
2 sets of 5 reps plus 1 contrast run with a 1-minute recovery between each rep and a 3-minute recovery between each set.

Variation/progression
5-yard explosive acceleration – the player covers 50 yards by alternating between acceleration and deceleration phases over distances of 5 yards. (NB: Quality not quantity is the key here!)

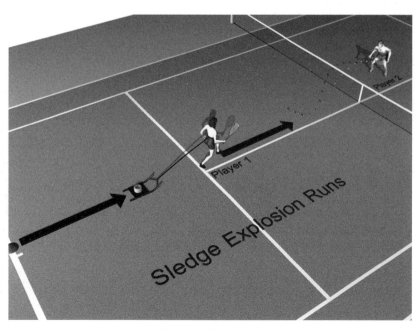

Figure 5.9 Sled running

DRILL

LATERAL POWER AND SPEED DEVELOPMENT

Aim

To develop explosive, controlled lateral ability; to develop precise and accurate catching of the ball at speed under pressure.

Area/equipment

Half a tennis court or an indoor or outdoor area. Tennis racket, Viper Belt with 2 Flexi-cords (1 attached at each side), 2 × 7.5-foot Fast Foot Ladders, tennis balls, 2 marker dots.

Description

Player 1 is connected to players 2 and 3 by the Viper Belt and 2 laterally fixed Flexi-cords. Player 4 stands on the other side of the court with the tennis balls. The ladders are placed along the service line 1 yard apart. Player 1 stands in the centre gap. Players 2 and 3 stand on the marker dots at either end of the ladders, providing resistance from both sides. The drill commences with player 4 serving the ball to either side of player 1, who moves laterally down the ladder under resistance from one side to return the ball. The drill continues in this manner for the required number of reps. When the reps have been completed the drill is performed without resistance (contrast phase). See Fig. 5.10.

Key teaching points

- Re-assert good arm mechanics when possible
- Maintain correct running form/mechanics
- Use short, explosive steps

Sets and reps

3 sets of 8 reps plus 2 contrast runs with a 3-minute recovery between each set.

Variations/progressions

- Perform the drill without the ladders
- Work in a sand pit or use high jump landing mats so player 1 can lunge and dive to return the ball
- Player 1 to wear a Side-Stepper; this will increase the resistance on the legs

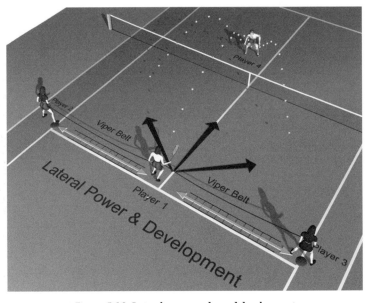

Figure 5.10 Lateral power and speed development

EXPLOSIVE

DRILL *EXPLOSIVE* *VERTICAL POWER DEVELOPMENT*

Aim

To develop vertical take-off power for the production of more air time and height when smashing the ball.

Area/equipment

Half a tennis court or an indoor or outdoor area. Tennis racket, tennis ball, Viper Belt with 2 Flexi-cords attached.

Description

Working in groups of 4, player 1 wears the Viper Belt, which has 1 looped Flexi-cord attached at each side. Players 2 and 3 stand a yard away, one on either side of the resisted player, standing on the Flexi-cords with their legs approximately 1 yard apart. Player 4 stands in front of the resisted player, throwing the ball above his/her head. The resisted player jumps to smash the ball before regaining position to repeat the drill. See Fig. 5.11.

Key teaching points

- Maintain correct jumping form/mechanics
- Do not sink into the hips, either before take-off or on landing
- Work off the balls of the feet
- On landing, regain balance before the next jump
- Perfect the timing of the jump

Sets and reps

3 sets of 8 reps plus 1 contrast jump with a 3-minute recovery between each set.

Variation/progression

Quick jumps – i.e. no repositioning between jumps. These are fast, repetitive jumps performed as quickly as possible.

Figure 5.11 Explosive vertical power development

DRILL

EXPLOSIVE LATERAL
MOVEMENT DEVELOPMENT

Aim
To develop explosive, co-ordinated and controlled lateral movement; to increase foot speed and improve foot-to-ground contact.

Area/equipment
Half a tennis court or an indoor or outdoor area. Tennis racket, tennis balls. 2 × 7.5-foot Fast Foot Ladders, Side-Stepper.

Description
The Fast Foot Ladders are placed along the service line with a 1-yard gap between them. Player 1, wearing the Side-Stepper adjusted so that the Flexi-cord is shorter between the ankles, stands in the gap between the 2 ladders. Player 2 stands 5 yards in front and throws tennis balls to the left and right of player 1, who moves laterally down the ladders using short, explosive steps to return the ball to player 2. See Fig. 5.12.

Key teaching points
- Work off the balls of the feet
- Use a strong arm and knee drive
- Try to keep a rhythmic skip
- Keep the head up, maintaining a good posture
- Use correct throwing and catching skills at all times

Sets and reps
3 sets of 6 reps with a 30-second recovery between each rep and a 2-minute recovery between each set.

Variations/progressions
- Player 2 uses 2 balls; after player 1 has returned the first ball, player 2 throws the second ball to the other side so that player 1 has to move across and attempt to return it. This makes the drill faster than when using just one ball
- 2 players stand at the end of a ladder. One calls for player 1 to move left or right in the ladders and then the other drops the ball. Player 1 has to move laterally then turn and explode onto the dropped ball

Figure 5.12 Explosive lateral movement development

DRILL MEDICINE BALL (JELLY BALL) WORKOUT

Aim
To develop explosive upper-body and core power.

Area/equipment
Half a tennis court or an indoor or outdoor area. Medicine balls (jelly balls) of various weights.

Description
Working in pairs or against a solid wall, players perform simple throws, e.g. chest passes, single arm passes, front slams, back slams, twist passes, woodchoppers and granny throws.

Key teaching points
- Start with a lighter ball for a warm-up set
- Start with simple movements before progressing to twists etc.
- Keep the spine upright
- Take care when loading (catching) and unloading (throwing) as this can put stress on the lower back

Sets and reps
1 set of 12 reps of each drill with a 1-minute recovery between each drill and a 3-minute recovery before the next exercise.

Variations/progressions
- Front slam
- Back slam
- Woodchopper
- Chest pass
- Single arm thrust
- Side slam
- Backward throw

Front slam

Back slam

Woodchopper

Chest pass

Single arm thrust

Side slam

Backward throw

DRILL **SHOT-SPECIFIC CLOSED STANCE**

Aim
To develop shot-specific power, strength and mobility for a closed stance forehand and backhand.

Area/equipment
An indoor or outdoor wall to work against. Jelly balls of various weights.

Description
With a closed stance, the player performs forehand and backhand throws against the wall, which should be 2 yards away.

Key teaching points
■ Take the ball to the back foot, simultaneously transferring body weight to the back foot
■ Transfer the weight and ball explosively forwards towards the wall
■ Thrust the hips forwards and work on the balls of the feet
■ Do not sink into the hips
■ Maintain a strong, upright core

Sets and reps
4 sets of 10 reps (2 sets forehand and 2 sets backhand) with a 1-minute recovery between each drill and a 3-minute recovery before the next exercise.

Variations/progressions
■ Vary the weight of the jelly balls used (3, 4 or 5 kg)
■ Change the weight of the jelly balls during the drill: start the drill with a heavy ball and finish with a lighter ball
■ Perform the last rep of each set with a light foam ball; this will increase the explosive speed of the stroke

DRILL — *MEDICINE BALL (JELLY BALL)*
SHOT-SPECIFIC OPEN STANCE

Aim
To develop shot-specific power, strength and mobility for an open stance forehand and backhand.

Area/equipment
An indoor or outdoor wall to work against. Jelly balls of various weights.

Description
With an open stance, the player performs forehand and backhand throws against the wall, which should be 2 yards away.

Key teaching points
- Rotate the shoulders, arms and ball past the right leg for the forehand and the left leg for the backhand (vice versa for left-handers)
- While transferring the ball, transfer the weight to the back foot
- Transfer the weight and ball towards the wall explosively by rotating the body
- Use the legs, then the hips, to transfer power

Sets and reps
4 sets of 10 reps (2 sets forehand and 2 sets backhand) with a 1-minute recovery between each drill and a 3-minute recovery before the next exercise.

Variations/progressions
- Vary the weight of the jelly balls used (3, 4 or 5 kg)
- Change the weight of the jelly balls during the drill: start the drill with a heavy ball and finish with a lighter ball
- Perform the last rep of each set with a light foam ball; this will increase the explosive speed of the stroke

DRILL

PLYOMETRICS –
LOW-IMPACT QUICK JUMPS

Aim
To develop explosive power for running, jumping and changing direction.

Area/equipment
Half a tennis court or an indoor or outdoor area. Fast Foot Ladder or marker dots placed 18 inches apart.

Description
The player performs double-footed single jumps, i.e. 1 jump between each rung. On reaching the end of the ladder, the player turns around and jumps back. See Fig. 5.13(a).

Key teaching points
- Maintain correct jumping form/mechanics
- The emphasis is on the speed of the jumps, but do not lose control – avoid feeling as though you are about to fall over the edge of a cliff when you reach the end of the drill
- Do not lean forwards too much

Sets and reps
2 sets of 2 reps with a 1-minute recovery between each set.

Variations/progressions
- Backwards jump
- Two jumps forwards and one back (see Fig. 5.13(b))
- Sideways jumps
- Sideways jumps, two one way and one back
- Hopscotch – 2 feet in one square and then 1 foot either side of the next square
- Left- and right-footed hops
- Increase the intensity – replace the Fast Foot Ladders or markers with 7- or 12-inch hurdles and perform the drills above

Figure 5.13(a) Low-impact quick jumps

Figure 5.13(b) Low-impact quick jumps – two forwards and one back

DRILL PLYOMETRIC CIRCUIT

Aim
To develop explosive multi-directional speed, agility and quickness.

Area/equipment
Half a tennis court or an indoor or outdoor area. Place Fast Foot Ladders, hurdles and marker dots in a circuit formation.

Description
Players jump, hop and zigzag their way through the circuit as stipulated by the coach. See Fig. 5.14.

Key teaching points
- Maintain the correct mechanics for each part of the circuit
- Ensure that there is a smooth transfer from running to jumping movements and vice versa

Sets and reps
5 circuits with a 1-minute recovery between each circuit.

Variation/progression
Work in pairs. Player 1 completes the circuit while player 2 feeds the ball in at various points around the circuit for player 1 to return.

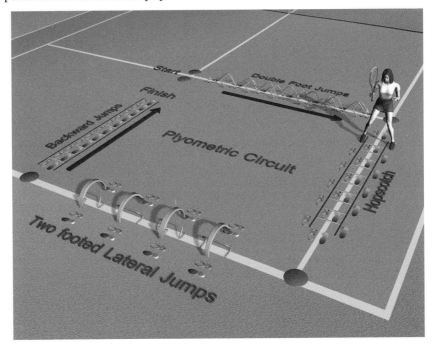

Figure 5.14 Plyometric circuit

DRILL   PLYOMETRICS – DROP JUMPS

Aim
To develop explosive multi-directional speed.

Area/equipment
Half a tennis court or an indoor or outdoor area with a cushioned or grassed landing surface. A stable platform or bench of variable height to jump from (15–36 inches depending on the stage of the season).

Description
Player stands on the platform and jumps off with feet together, lands on the balls of the feet then accelerates away for 5 yards.

Key teaching points
- Do not land flat-footed
- Do not sink into the hips on landing
- Maintain a strong core
- Keep the head up – this will help to align the spine

Sets and reps
2 sets of 10 reps with a 3-minute recovery between each set.

Variations/progressions
- Backwards drop jumps
- Side drop jumps
- Drop jumps with a mid-air twist
- Include a ball for the players to accelerate on to

DRILL   *EXPLOSIVE GROUND REACTIONS*

Aim
To develop multi-directional explosive movements.

Area/equipment
Half a tennis court or a hard-surfaced indoor or outdoor area. Reaction ball. The drill can also be performed against a wall.

Description
Players work in pairs or individually against a wall. The reaction ball is thrown to land within 1 yard of the player, who attempts to catch it before the second bounce. The ball is shaped so that it will bounce off the surface at different angles and different heights, forcing the player to react accordingly.

Key teaching points
- Bend at the knees, not at the waist
- Work off the balls of the feet
- Keep the hands in front of the body, ready to react
- The ball should not be thrown hard – it will do the necessary work itself

Sets and reps
3 sets of 25 reps with a 1-minute recovery between each set.

Variations/progressions
- Vary the starting position
- Use rackets

DRILL   WEIGHTED RACKET

Aim
To develop upper-body strength, power and speed.

Area/equipment
Half a tennis court or an indoor or outdoor area. Tennis racket, tennis ball. The tennis racket can be weighted by strapping ankle weights around the upper handle or attaching weights to the strings etc. (see Fig. 5.15). Work with 1–1.5 lb weights.

Description
Player plays a full range of shots with the weighted tennis racket for 30 seconds, then repeats with a normal, unweighted racket for 15 seconds (contrast phase).

Key teaching points
- It is important to stick closely to the sets and reps
- Always perform a contrast shot

Sets and reps
5 sets of 8 × 30 seconds with 1 × 15-second contrast.

Variations/progressions
- Vary sets and reps
- Vary the weight on the tennis racket

Weighted Band

Figure 5.15 Weighted racket

Aim
To develop game-specific explosive footwork patterns.

Area/equipment
Full tennis court or an indoor or outdoor area. 2 Side-Steppers, tennis racket, tennis balls.

Description
Players, wearing Side-Steppers, play a normal practice game (see Fig. 5.16). After every 30 seconds the Side-Steppers are removed and a contrast phase of 10–15 seconds is completed before the Side-Steppers are put back on.

Key teaching points
- Work on the balls of the feet
- Use quick, powerful foot movements
- Stay tall
- Do not sink into the hips

Sets and reps
30 seconds with resistance then 10–15 seconds contrast. Repeat for 2 games.

Variation/progression
Use a weighted racket as well as the Side-Steppers.

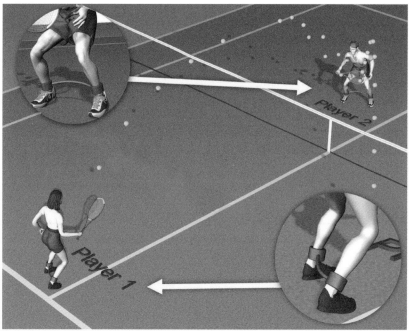

Figure 5.16 Game-specific explosive footwork development

| DRILL | *ASSISTED RESISTED*
BASE LINE TO NET RUNNING |

Aim
To develop acceleration, explosive turns and re-acceleration for running base line to net, net to base line.

Area/equipment
Half a tennis court or an indoor or outdoor area. Tennis racket, tennis ball, Viper Belt.

Description
Player 1, wearing the Viper Belt so that the Flexi-cord is attached at the front (belly button), stands behind the base line. Player 2, who is attached to the safety harness, facing player 1, stands in the centre of the court and begins to walk down towards the net. Player 1 will feel the resistance of the Flexi-cord. After player 2 has covered 3–4 yards, player 1 accelerates towards the net. This is the overspeed phase. Player 2 now changes direction and starts walking towards the base line. As player 1 gets nearer, the net resistance will kick in. On reaching the net he/she turns and accelerates back to the base line, once again under assistance from the Flexi-cord. The drill is completed when player 1 reaches the base line and player 2 has begun moving back to centre court. The action is best described as a 'whiplash' motion with player 2 controlling the handle with player 1 at the end of the line. See Fig. 5.17.

Key teaching points
- Maintain correct running form/mechanics
- Use short steps before and after the turn

Sets and reps
3 sets of 3 runs with 1 contrast run at the end of each set; a 30-second recovery at the end of each run and a 2-minute recovery at the end of each set.

Variation/progression
Vary starting positions, i.e. side-on, backwards etc.

Figure 5.17 Assisted resisted base line to net running

DRILL   ASSISTED RESISTED TOW RUNS

Aim
To develop explosive running.

Area/equipment
Full tennis court or an indoor or outdoor area. Tennis racket. Viper Belt.

Description
Players 1 and 2 are attached to each other by the Viper Belt. Player 1 runs away from player 2, who stands still until the resistance is strong, then is pulled forwards. This acceleration is assisted. Player 1 now decelerates until he/she feels the resistance from behind diminish, then accelerates again under resistance. The procedure is repeated for the length of the court.

Key teaching points
■ Maintain correct running form/mechanics
■ Both players should use a strong arm drive
■ Both players should use short steps during the acceleration and deceleration phases

Sets and reps
2 sets of 6 reps with a 30-second recovery between each rep and a 2-minute recovery between each set.

Variation/progression
Vary starting positions.

TEAM GAMES IN PREPARATION FOR THE NEXT LEVEL

This stage is quite short in duration, but very important, as it brings together all the elements of the SAQ Continuum into highly competitive, and even enjoyable, situations involving other players. Short, high-intensity tag-type games and random agility tests work well here.

The key is for players to be fired up – to perform fast, explosive and controlled movements that leave them exhilarated and mentally and physically ready for the next stage in training or the next game.

DRILL   BRITISH BULLDOG

Aim
To practise multi-directional explosive movements in a pressured situation.

Area/equipment
Half a tennis court or an indoor or outdoor area of approximately 20 square yards. 20 marker dots to mark out start and finish lines.

Description
One player is nominated and stands in the centre of the grid, while the rest stand to one side behind the start line. On the coach's call, all the players attempt to get to the opposite side of the square without being caught by the player in the middle. When the player in the middle captures another player, he/she joins them in the middle and helps to capture more 'prisoners'. See Fig. 6.1.

Key teaching points
■ Use correct mechanics at all times
■ Keep the head and eyes up to avoid collisions with other players

Sets and reps
Play British Bulldog for approximately 3–4 minutes before moving on to the more technical aspects of the game.

Variation/progression
The player in the middle uses a tennis ball to touch other players in order to capture them. The ball can be held or thrown.

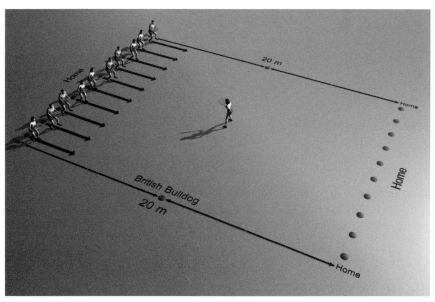

Figure 6.1 British Bulldog

DRILL | CIRCLE BALL

Aim
To practise using explosive evasion skills.

Area/equipment
Half a tennis court or an indoor or outdoor area. Tennis balls. Players make a circle about 15 yards in diameter (depending on the size of the group).

Description
1 or 2 players stand in the centre of the circle while the players on the outside have 1 or 2 balls. The object is for those on the outside to try and make contact (with the ball) with those on the inside. The players on the inside try to dodge the balls. The winners are the pair with the least number of hits during their time in the centre. See Fig. 6.2.

Key teaching point
Players on the inside should use the correct mechanics.

Sets and reps
Each pair to stay in the centre area for 45 seconds.

Variation/progression
Players in the middle have to hold on to each other's hand or use a Break-Away Belt.

Figure 6.2 Circle ball

DRILL ROBBING THE NEST

Aim
To practise multi-directional explosive speed, agility and quickness.

Area/equipment
Half a tennis court or an indoor or outdoor area. Using marker dots, mark out a large outer circle about 25 yards in diameter and an inner circle measuring 2 yards in diameter. Place a number of balls in the inner circle.

Description
2 nominated players defend the 'nest' of tennis balls with the rest of the players standing outside the outer circle (the 'safe zone'). The game starts when the outside players run in and try to steal the tennis balls from the nest, then run back to the safe zone. The 2 defenders try to prevent the robbers from getting the tennis balls to the safe zone by tagging them or getting in their way. For every successful tag and prevention, the ball is returned to the centre circle. See Fig. 6.3.

Key teaching points
- Correct mechanics must be used at all times
- Players should dodge, swerve, weave, side-step, etc.
- Light contact only should be used

Sets and reps
Each pair to defend for about 45 seconds.

Variation/progression
Defenders work together either by holding hands or interlocking arms; the defenders will have to work hard to prevent the robbers.

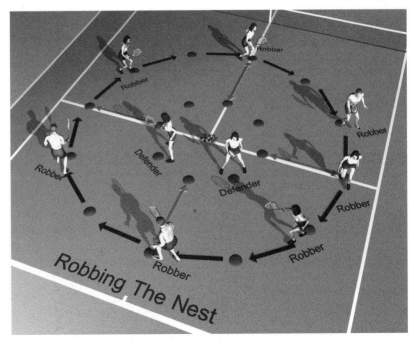

Figure 6.3 Robbing the nest

DRILL ODD ONE OUT

Aim
To practise speed, agility and quickness in a competitive environment.

Area/equipment
Half a tennis court or an indoor or outdoor area. Marker dots, tennis balls. Mark out an outer circle 20–25 yards in diameter and an inner circle about 2 yards in diameter.

Description
Place a number of tennis balls in the centre area, 1 fewer than the number of players present. The players are situated on the outside of the outer circle. On the coach's call, they start running around the outer circle; on the coach's second call, they collect a ball from the inner circle as quickly as possible. The player without a ball is out and performs a tennis skill drill as directed by the coach. The coach then removes another ball and repeats the process until there is only one player left. See Fig. 6.4.

Key teaching points
■ Correct mechanics must be used at all times
■ Players should be aware of other players around them

Sets and reps
Play the game until a winner emerges.

Variation/progression
Work in pairs, joined together by holding hands or using a Break-Away Belt, with 1 ball between 2 players. If a pair break away from each other, they are disqualified.

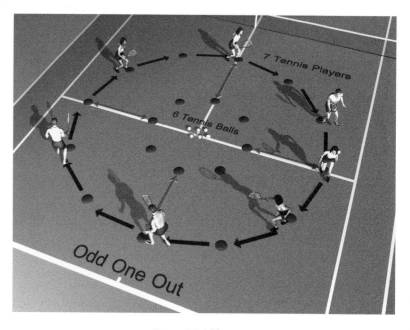

Figure 6.4 Odd one out

DRILL *MARKER TURNS*

Aim
To practise multi-directional speed, agility and quickness.

Area/equipment
Half a tennis court or an indoor or outdoor area. 50 small markers. Place the markers in and around the half court; 25 of the markers should be turned upside-down and 25 should be the right way around.

Description
Working in two small teams (2–3 players per team), one team attempts to turn over the upright markers and the other team attempts to turn over the upside-down markers. The winners are the team that has the largest number of markers their way around after 60 seconds. See Fig. 6.5.

Key teaching points
■ Initiate a good arm drive after turning a marker
■ Use correct multi-directional mechanics
■ Be aware of other players around the area

Sets and reps
A game should last for 60 seconds.

Variation/progression
Use 4 teams and 4 different-coloured markers.

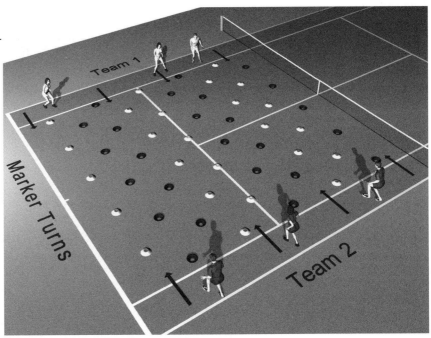

Figure 6.5 Marker turns

DRILL | *DODGE BALL*

Aim
To practise explosive lateral speed, agility and quickness.

Area/equipment
Half a tennis court or an indoor or outdoor walled area. Bag of tennis balls.

Description
Working in small groups (from 3 to 7 or 8 players per group), 1 player stands in front of the group with the bag of tennis balls 5–10 yards away. The others face the single player, who starts to throw the balls underarm in an attempt to hit the players. The players try to dodge the balls by moving explosively in different lateral directions. If they are hit they are out of the game. See Fig. 6.6.

Key teaching points
- Use correct multi-directional mechanics
- Use a strong arm drive when moving laterally
- Keep the hips square for as long as possible before turning
- Use short, explosive steps
- Be aware of other players around the area

Sets and reps
Each game to last 2 minutes with a 1-minute recovery between games. Swap the ball thrower for each new game.

Variation/progression
Dodgers to work in pairs by holding hands or linking arms.

Figure 6.6 Dodge ball

CHAPTER 7   VISION AND REACTION

Many people involved in tennis who have 20/20 vision assume that their visual ability for the sport will be competent. Most eye tests only give us results for static visual acuity, which is simply the ability to identify certain black letters on the white background of an eye chart. However, tennis players use a whole range of visual abilities whenever decisions need to be made and movements into areas need to be completed, particularly when getting into position to return a tennis ball, tracking the tennis ball on court and visually assessing the opponent's movements and position.

The following drills will help in the areas of:

Dynamic visual acuity – the ability to maintain the clarity of an object while moving.

Colour vision – simply the ability to recognise the various colours of the spectrum.

Depth perception – the ability to judge distances rapidly and accurately.

Visual reaction time – the time required to perceive and respond to visual stimulation.

Central–peripheral awareness – the ability to pay attention to what you are looking at, yet to be aware of what is going on peripherally around you without moving your eyes and losing the central focus.

Eye–hand–body co-ordination – the ability to integrate the eyes, hands and body as a whole unit.

DRILL   EYE–HAND REACTION DEVELOPMENT

Aim
To develop fast, accurate hand/racket skills; to develop visual skills, including colour vision and visual reaction time.

Area/equipment
Half a tennis court or an indoor or outdoor area. Tennis racket, Visual Acuity Ring.

Description
Working in pairs, player 1 throws the ring so that it rotates in the air to player 2. Prior to throwing, player 1 nominates one of the coloured balls attached to the ring for player 2 to visually track and catch. Gradually increase the speed of the spin on the Visual Acuity Ring as proficiency improves. See Fig. 7.1.

Key teaching points
- Keep the head still – move the eyes to track the ring
- Work off the balls of the feet at all times
- The hands should be out and in front of the body, ready to catch the ring

Sets and reps
2 sets of 20 reps with a 1-minute recovery between each set.

Variations/progressions
- Turn and catch
- Throw the ring sideways
- Instead of catching the ball on the ring, hit it with a racket

Figure 7.1 Eye–hand reaction

DRILL   *PERIPHERAL AWARENESS*

Aim
To develop peripheral awareness; to help the player detect and react to a ball coming from behind and from the side more quickly.

Area/equipment
Half a tennis court or an indoor or outdoor area. Tennis racket, Peripheral Vision Stick.

Description
Work in pairs with player 1 behind player 2, who stands in a ready position. Player 1 holds the stick and moves it from behind player 2 into his/her field of vision. As soon as player 2 detects the stick, he/she claps both hands over the ball at the end of the stick or hits the ball with a racket. See Fig. 7.2.

Key teaching points
- Player 2 should work off the balls of the feet and in a slightly crouched position with the hands held out ready (an athletic position)
- Player 1 must be careful not to touch any part of player 2's body with the stick
- Player 1 should vary the speed at which the stick is brought into player 2's field of vision

Sets and reps
2 set of 20 reps with no recovery between each rep and a 1-minute recovery between each set.

Variations/progressions
- Instead of using a Peripheral Vision Stick, throw tennis balls from behind player 2 for him/her to fend off
- Use 2 Peripheral Vision Sticks; as one is brought into player 2's vision, use the other stick on the other side. Player 2 has to respond quickly with two movements

Figure 7.2 Peripheral awareness

DRILL   REACTOR BALL

Aim
To develop lightning-quick reactions.

Area/equipment
Half a tennis court or an indoor or outdoor area, but not a grass surface. Reactor Ball (see Fig. 7.3) or rugby ball.

Description
Work in pairs standing 5 yards apart. Player 1 throws the ball so that it lands in front of player 2; because of the structure of the ball it will bounce in any direction. Player 2 has to react and catch the ball before it bounces for a second time.

Figure 7.3 Reactor balls

Key teaching points
■ The player catching the ball should work off the balls of the feet and in a slightly crouched position with the hands out ready
■ The ball should not be thrown hard – it will do the necessary work itself

Sets and reps
2 sets of 20 reps with no recovery between each rep and a 1-minute recovery between each set.

Variations/progressions
■ Work individually or in pairs by throwing the ball against a wall
■ Players to stand on agility discs while throwing the ball to each other

DRILL   *BUNT BAT*

Aim
To develop lightning-quick hand–eye co-ordination.

Area/equipment
Half a tennis court or an indoor or outdoor area. Bunt Bat. Tennis balls or beanbags.

Description
Work in pairs; one of the players holds the Bunt Bat. The partner stands about 3–4 yards away and throws a ball or beanbag, simultaneously calling the colour of one of the balls on the Bunt Bat. The other player's task is to fend off the ball/beanbag with the appropriate coloured ball on the Bunt Bat. See Fig. 7.4.

Key teaching points
■ Start throwing the balls/beanbags slowly and gradually build up speed
■ The player should be in a get-set position

Sets and reps
3 sets of 25 reps with a 30-second recovery between each set.

Variations/progressions
■ Use different coloured balls/beanbags – when the ball/beanbag has been thrown, it is to be fended off with the corresponding coloured ball on the Bunt Bat
■ The player with the Bunt Bat stands on an agility disc while performing the drill

Figure 7.4 Bunt Bat

DRILL   *FOLLOW THE THUMB*

Aim
To develop all-round and peripheral vision.

Area/equipment
Half a tennis court or an indoor or outdoor area.

Description
Hold either arm out in front and make the 'thumbs up' sign. Keeping your head still and only moving your eyes, move the thumb up, down and around, following it with your eyes. Make sure you are moving to the extremes of your range of vision. Start slowly and gradually increase the speed of the movement.

Key teaching points
- Sit or stand upright with good posture
- Try the drill with both hands
- Keep the head still – do not move it
- Only move your eyes

Sets and reps
5 sets of 1 minute with a 30-second recovery between each set.

Variations/progressions
- While performing the drill, get another player to throw you a tennis ball to catch and return: do this once in each set
- Perform the drill while standing on an agility disc

DRILL *TRACKING AND FOCUS*

Aim
To develop ball-tracking ability and to make subtle focus adjustments.

Area/equipment
Half a tennis court or an indoor or outdoor area. Tennis racket, tennis balls.

Description
Draw numbers or letters on 4 sides of the ball – use black ink on white/yellow balls (see Fig. 7.5). 2 players stand 10–15 yards apart. Player 1 holds up the ball for 2 seconds so that a number is clearly facing player 2. Player 2 calls out the number as the ball is served, and then returns the ball by playing the necessary stroke. The drill is now reversed.

Figure 7.5 Tracking and focus

Key teaching points
■ Keep the head still
■ Move the eyes, not the head

Sets and reps
5 sets of 12 reps with a 30-second recovery between each set.

Variations/progressions
■ Vary the time the ball is held up for
■ Vary the distance between the players
■ Vary the angle the ball is served at

DRILL | DYNAMIC VISUAL ACUITY TRAINING

Aim

To develop ball-tracking ability while in motion; this drill also assists the ability to focus on an opponent while he/she is in action.

Area/equipment

Half a tennis court or an indoor or outdoor area. Tennis racket, 8 tennis balls.

Description

Number the balls 1–8, ensuring that ball 1 has the figure 1 marked on 6 sides of the ball and so on. Use black ink on white/yellow balls. 2 players stand 10–15 yards apart. Player 1 holds a ball so that player 2 cannot see what number is on it, then throws it towards player 2, who calls out what number ball has been thrown while it is in the air before hitting the ball back. Player 1 should throw the balls to player 2 in a random order. See Fig. 7.6.

Key teaching points

■ Keep the head still
■ Move the eyes, not the head
■ Maintain an athletic position
■ Work on the balls of the feet

Sets and reps

5 sets of 12 reps with a 30-second recovery between each set.

Variations/progressions

■ Vary the distance between the players
■ Vary the angle at which the ball is thrown
■ Each player has 4 balls and they alternate the call/throw between them
■ Work on a full court; the player receiving the ball stands on the base line and calls out the number on the ball before returning it

Figure 7.6 Dynamic visual acuity training

DRILL BALL PLACEMENT DECISION MAKING

Aim
To develop quick ball placement decision making.

Area/equipment
Half a tennis court or an indoor or outdoor area. Tennis racket, bag of multi-coloured tennis balls.

Description
Use a bag of 3 different-coloured tennis balls, i.e. yellow, red and white. The two players decide which colour ball represents which side of the court the ball has to be returned to, i.e. white balls have to be returned to the left of the court, red to the middle and yellow to the right. Player 1 throws the ball to player 2 who, on recognising the colour, returns the ball to the agreed side of the court. Roles are reversed on completion of the drill.

Key teaching points
- Keep the head still; move the eyes only
- Maintain an athletic position
- Ensure that the ball is delivered quickly, forcing the receiving player to identify the colour of the ball while it is in the air

Sets and reps
1 bag of balls per player equals one set.

Variations/progressions
- Vary the distance between the players
- Vary the angle at which the ball is served
- Vary the speed of delivery

DRILL *FAST HANDS*

Aim
To develop lightning-quick hand reactions.

Area/equipment
Half a tennis court or an indoor or outdoor area.

Description
Working in pairs, player 1 puts his/her hands together and holds them slightly away in front of the chest. Player 2 stands directly in front with his/her hands held at the sides. The drill begins with player 2 attempting to slap player 1's hands. Player 1 tries to prevent player 2 by moving his/her hands away as quickly as possible. Players alternate roles.

Key teaching points
- Stand in an athletic position
- Keep the head still

Sets and reps
30 seconds each per drill.

Variations/progressions
- Player 1 holds his/her hands out with the palms facing the ground, the tips of the thumbs just touching. Player 2 holds his/her hands just above. The drill commences with player 2 attempting to slap both of player 1's hands before player 1 can react by moving them away
- Player 1 stands directly in front of player 2, 1 or 2 yards away. Player 1 jabs a punch at player 2, who attempts to clap both hands over the fist

CHAPTER 8

BALANCE, CO-ORDINATION, FEEL AND JUDGEMENT

Other important physical attributes required by tennis players include the ability to be balanced and well co-ordinated in all movements, and the physical and spatial awareness (feel) needed to transfer power in a game that places ever-changing demands on the individual. During a rally a player explodes to the net, then stops in an instant with tremendous balance and co-ordination before lunging forwards with power and grace to hit the ball with a soft touch, leaving the opponent stranded on the base line. All of these skills can be trained and developed over a period of time.

DRILL FEEL AND DISTANCE

Aim
To develop feel and judgement of distance while manipulating objects of different weights and different sizes.

Area/equipment
Half a tennis court or an indoor or outdoor area. 4 bins, waste-paper baskets or small pop-up nets. Assorted golf balls, foam balls, plastic balls, tennis balls, cricket balls, hockey balls, beanbags and fly balls.

Description
4 baskets are placed in a line 5 metres apart with a mixture of balls in the first basket. Player picks out any ball and throws it into one of the baskets, then selects a different ball or beanbag and attempts to throw it into the same basket as the first ball. This sequence is continued until the basket of balls is empty. See Fig. 8.1.

Key teaching points
■ Stand in an athletic position
■ Keep the head still

Sets and reps
Perform the drill until the basket of balls is empty.

Variations/progressions
■ Vary the standing position, i.e. side on
■ Work in pairs. Player 1 picks a ball out of the first basket and passes it to player 2, who then throws it into the other basket

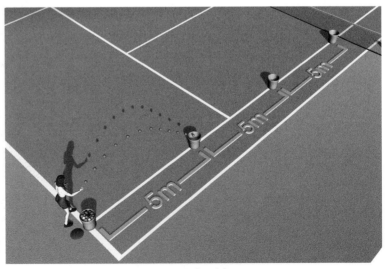

Figure 8.1 Feel and distance

DRILL   JUGGLING VARIOUS BALLS ON RACKET

Aim
To develop feel and judgement while manipulating balls of different sizes and weights.

Area/equipment
Half a tennis court or an indoor or outdoor area. Tennis racket. Different types of balls including tennis, foam, hard rubber, golf, cricket, hockey, fly etc.

Description
Working in pairs, player 1 juggles a ball on his/her racket for 10 seconds; player 2 then introduces a different ball for player 1 to juggle while the other ball is allowed to drop to the ground. This is continued with a number of various balls. See Fig. 8.2.

Key teaching points
- Stand in an athletic position
- Keep the head still
- Work on the balls of the feet

Sets and reps
3 sets of 2 minutes with a 30-second recovery between each set.

Variations/progressions
- Work in pairs, hitting the different balls to each other
- Walk and run while juggling the ball

Figure 8.2 Juggling various balls on racket

DRILL TOUCH AND AWARENESS

Aim
To develop touch, feel, awareness of contact and control in different environments.

Area/equipment
Full tennis court or an indoor or outdoor area. Various modified tennis rackets (i.e. loose strings, hard strings), solid round bat, squash racket, rackets with different surfaces applied (i.e. sheet of rubber, hardboard, felt etc.). The idea is to change the surface and feel of the racket.

Description
Place the rackets on the floor on one side of the base line. Working in a group, players line up just outside the court. The coach or another player delivers a ball from the other side of the court; the first player of the group will run, pick up one of the rackets and play a shot, then return the racket to the end of the line of other rackets. The next player will then pick up the next racket, which will have a different surface, and play the next shot. This is continued until all of the group have played a number of shots with different rackets.

Key teaching point
Start in an athletic position.

Sets and reps
5 sets of 2 minutes with a 30-second recovery between each set.

Variations/progressions
- Vary the starting position, i.e. side on
- Place a line of rackets on each side of the net, and work in 2 groups playing a rally

DRILL   LILY-PAD DRILL

Aim
To develop dynamic balance, co-ordination and proprioception.

Area/equipment
Half a tennis court or an indoor or outdoor area. Tennis rackets, tennis balls, 8 agility discs.

Description
Place the agility discs in a staggered line so that players can walk from one agility disc to another. Player 1 stands 4 or 5 yards away. Player 2 starts the drill by walking down the row of agility discs; player 1 serves the ball for player 2 to return while balancing on the discs. See Fig. 8.3.

Key teaching points
- Start in an athletic position
- Maintain a strong core
- Look up and focus on ball, not the agility discs
- Do not sink into the hips

Sets and reps
3 sets of 3 reps with a 30-second recovery between each set.

Variations/progressions
- Perform the drill laterally
- Increase the distance between the agility discs, therefore changing the player's stance

Figure 8.3 Lily-pad drill

DRILL | BALANCE BEAM WALK

Aim
To develop proprioception, balance and co-ordination.

Area/equipment
Half a tennis court or an indoor or outdoor area. Tennis racket, tennis balls. Balance beam.

Description
Place a balance beam on the ground in the centre-court area. Player 1 stands 4 or 5 yards away; player 2 commences the drill by standing on the balance beam and gradually walking down it. Player 1 then serves the ball to player 2, who hits the ball back to player 1. This is continued for the length of the balance beam. See Fig. 8.4.

Key teaching points
- Start in an athletic position
- Maintain a strong core
- Look up and focus on the ball, not the balance beam
- Do not sink in to the hips

Sets and reps
3 sets of 3 reps with a 30-second recovery between sets.

Variation/progression
Perform the drill laterally.

Figure 8.4 Balance beam walk

DRILL *MINI TRAMPOLINE MANIPULATIONS*

Aim
To develop proprioception, balance, co-ordination and manipulation skills.

Area/equipment
Half a tennis court or an indoor or outdoor area. Tennis racket, tennis balls. Mini trampoline.

Description
Player stands on the mini trampoline with a racket and ball and gradually starts to rebound while juggling the ball with the racket. The player should increase his/her speed as confidence and skills improve. See Fig. 8.5(a).

Key teaching points
- Start in an athletic position
- Maintain a strong core
- Do not sink in to the hips

Sets and reps
3 sets of 2 minutes with a 30-second recovery between each set.

Variation/progression
Work in pairs. Player A rebounds while player B delivers a ball for player A to return. See Fig. 8.5(b).

Figure 8.5(a) Mini trampoline manipulations

Figure 8.5(b) Mini trampoline manipulations – in pairs

CHAPTER 9

TENNIS–SPECIFIC COMPLEX WEIGHTS PROGRAMME

The following tennis-specific weights programme is ideal for all players. It is simple, basic and time efficient.

It has been developed to improve whole-body muscular strength and dynamic explosive power. There is a focus on core stabilisation and upper-body proprioception, including functional and tennis-specific movements.

It is simple to implement: you don't need to attend a gym or depend on machines and an array of weights. All you need is a set of adjustable dumbbells (5–12 kg per dumbbell), a 55 or 65 cm core stability ball and a 5 kg jelly ball. The equipment is easily transportable and fits into the boot of a car, so can be transported to away matches.

The 'wave' weight programme is so-called because the reps move up and down. The object is to slightly increase the weight lifted when the reps are lower, so that the next time you perform a higher number of reps you will be lifting more weight. The programme sheet can be copied so you can monitor your lifts in the space provided. Work to failure, then recover and commence the next set without compromising good technique. Complete the programme at least twice a week, preferably when fresh.

Before beginning the programme, warm up and mobilise your body by completing a set of the exercises with no or very light weights. This will prepare your body for the hard work to come.

DRILL   CORE BALL DUMBBELL PRESS (1A)

Description
Stabilise yourself on the core ball. Press the dumbbells overhead, then lower. Maintain the tempo of 4 seconds down, 2 seconds up.

Key teaching points
- Maintain a strong base; tighten your core muscles and maintain throughout the exercise
- Keep your hips up and squeeze your gluteal muscles throughout
- Maintain a smooth, continuous action
- Do not lock out your elbows
- Remember to breathe out on the effort

DRILL   HAND-CLAP PRESS-UP (1B) – COMPLEX

Description
Get into a press-up position. Lower your chest to the floor, then push back up explosively, clapping your hands before getting back into the start position.

Key teaching points
- Try to maintain good body alignment throughout
- Make sure you cushion your impact and set yourself in between each repetition

DRILL SINGLE-LEG DUMBBELL SQUAT (2A)

Description
Holding a dumbbell in each hand, perform a single-leg squat.

Key teaching points
- Maintain balance and stability throughout
- Look ahead and focus
- Keep your back straight and your core muscles tight
- Remember to breathe out on the effort

DRILL SINGLE-LEG JUMP SMASH (2B)

Description
Perform single-leg jumps on alternate legs, while your partner delivers a ball for you to smash in the 'up' position.

Key teaching points
- Maintain balance and stability throughout
- Keep your back straight and your core muscles tight

DRILL CORE BALL UPRIGHT PRESS (3A)

Description
Stabilise yourself on the core ball. Press the dumbbells overhead, then lower. Maintain the tempo of 4 seconds down, 2 seconds up.

Key teaching points
- Maintain a good base; tighten your core muscles and maintain throughout the exercise
- Maintain a smooth, continuous action
- Do not lock out your elbows
- Remember to breathe out on the effort

DRILL *CORE BALL* JELLY BALL THROW (3B) – COMPLEX

Description
Stabilise yourself on the core ball. Press the jelly ball over your head with an explosive action, rebounding the ball off a wall.

Key teaching points
- Maintain a good base throughout; tighten your core muscles and maintain throughout the exercise
- Control each throw

DRILL · ANGLED DUMBBELL LUNGE (4)

Description
Stand in an upright position in an athletic stance, feet shoulder-width apart and knees slightly bent. Holding the dumbbells by your sides, lunge forwards with alternate legs so that your knee bends to a 45-degree angle.

Key teaching points
- Maintain good posture and alignment throughout
- Control the lunge on the way down, then 'snap' back to the return position

CORE BALL
DRILL · SINGLE-ARM BENT-OVER ROW (5)

Description
Adopt a good, stable position on the core ball with a dumbbell in one hand. Pull the dumbbell into your side, leading with the elbow, then lower. Alternate arms.

Key teaching points
- Keep your back straight and tighten your core muscles throughout
- Do not twist
- Keep your head up
- Maintain a smooth, continuous action

WEIGHTS PROGRAMME

EXERCISE ORDER		SESSION 1	SESSION 2	SESSION 3	SESSION 4	SESSION 5	SESSION 6	SESSION 7	SESSION 8	SESSION 9
1A Core ball dumbbell press	Weight									
	Sets and reps	3 × 8	3 × 7	3 × 6	3 × 7	3 × 8	3 × 9	3 × 7	3 × 6	3 × 7
	Speed	4 down 2 up	4 down 2 up	4 down 2 up	4 down 2 up	4 down 2 up	4 down 2 up	4 down 2 up	4 down 2 up	4 down 2 up
	Recovery	30 sec	30 sec	30 sec	30 sec	2 min	2 min	2 min	2 min	2 min
After each set of reps, move immediately to the next drill within the specified time. Return to commence the next set.										
1B Hand-clap press-up	Weight									
	Sets and reps	2 × 8	2 × 7	2 × 6	2 × 7	2 × 8	2 × 9	2 × 7	2 × 6	2 × 7
	Speed									
	Recovery	2 min	2 min	2 min	2 min	2 min	2 min	2 min	2 min	2 min
After each set of reps, move immediately to the next drill within the specified time. Return to commence the next set.										
2A Single-leg dumbbell squat	Weight									
	Sets and reps	3 × 7 × 7	3 × 8 × 8	3 × 9 × 9	3 × 5 × 5	3 × 6 × 6	3 × 7 × 7	3 × 9 × 9	3 × 5 × 5	3 × 8 × 8
	Speed	4 down 2 up	4 down 2 up	4 down 2 up	4 down 2 up	4 down 2 up	4 down 2 up	4 down 2 up	4 down 2 up	4 down 2 up
	Recovery	30 sec	30 sec	30 sec	30 sec	30 sec	30 sec	30 sec	30 sec	30 sec
After each set of reps, move immediately to the next drill within the specified time. Return to commence the next set.										
2B Single-leg jump smash	Weight									
	Sets and reps	3 × 5 × 5	3 × 6 × 6	3 × 4 × 4	3 × 6 × 6	3 × 7 × 7	3 × 5 × 5	3 × 8 × 8	3 × 7 × 7	3 × 9 × 9
	Speed									
	Recovery	2 min	2 min	2 min	2 min	2 min	2 min	2 min	2 min	2 min

EXERCISE ORDER		SESSION 1	SESSION 2	SESSION 3	SESSION 4	SESSION 5	SESSION 6	SESSION 7	SESSION 8	SESSION 9
3A Core ball upright press	Weight									
	Sets and reps	3 × 9	3 × 8	3 × 7	3 × 10	3 × 12	3 × 10	3 × 8	3 × 10	3 × 12
	Speed	4 down 2 up	4 down 2 up	4 down 2 up	4 down 2 up	4 down 2 up	4 down 2 up	4 down 2 up	4 down 2 up	4 down 2 up
	Recovery	1 min	1 min	1 min	1 min	1 min	1 min	1 min	1 min	1 min
After each set of reps, move immediately to the next drill within the specified time. Return to commence the next set.										
3B Core ball jelly ball throw	Weight	5 kg	5 kg	5 kg	5 kg	5 kg	5 kg	5 kg	5 kg	5 kg
	Sets and reps	3 × 10	3 × 8	3 × 6	3 × 8	3 × 12	3 × 10	3 × 8	3 × 12	3 × 10
	Speed									
	Recovery	2 min	2 min	2 min	2 min	2 min	2 min	2 min	2 min	2 min
4 Angled dumbbell lunge	Weight									
	Sets and reps	3 × 6 × 6	3 × 8 × 8	3 × 10 × 10	3 × 7 × 7	3 × 6 × 6	3 × 8 × 8	3 × 9 × 9	3 × 10 × 10	3 × 7 × 7
	Speed	Control down, quick back								
	Recovery	2 min	2 min	2 min	2 min	2 min	2 min	2 min	2 min	2 min
5 Core ball single-arm bent-over row	Weight									
	Sets and reps	3 × 8 × 8	3 × 10 × 10	3 × 8 × 8	3 × 7 × 7	3 × 9 × 9	3 × 10 × 10	3 × 12 × 12	3 × 8 × 8	3 × 9 × 9
	Speed	4 down 2 up	4 down 2 up	4 down 2 up	4 down 2 up	4 down 2 up	4 down 2 up	4 down 2 up	4 down 2 up	4 down 2 up
	Recovery	3 min	3 min	3 min	3 min	3 min	3 min	3 min	3 min	3 min

CHAPTER 10
WARM–DOWN, RECOVERY AND FLEXIBILITY

Due to the intense activity levels reached during the main part of the session, time should be set aside for a warm-down to reduce the heart rate gradually to near resting levels. This will help to:

■ disperse lactic acid

■ prevent blood pooling

■ return the body systems to normal levels

■ assist in recovery

■ develop and maintain flexibility.

The structure of the warm-down will essentially be the reverse of the Dynamic Flex warm-up, and will last for approximately 5 minutes depending on the fitness level of the players. It begins with moderate Dynamic Flex movements, and will then gradually become less intense and smaller in amplitude. These exercises should still focus on quality of movement (good mechanics).

DRILL HIGH KNEE-LIFT SKIP

Follow the instructions on page 15.

Aim
To warm down the hips and buttocks gradually.

Sets and reps
2 × 22 yards, 1 forwards and 1 backwards.

Intensity
60 per cent for the first 11 yards and 50 per cent for the second 11 yards.

DRILL KNEE-ACROSS SKIP

Follow the instructions on page 16.

Aim
To warm down the hip flexors gradually by lowering the intensity of the exercise.

Sets and reps
2 × 22 yards, 1 forwards and 1 backwards.

Intensity
50 per cent for the first 11 yards and 40 per cent for the second 11 yards.

DRILL WIDE SKIP

Follow the instructions on page 12.

Aim
To warm down the hips and ankles.

Sets and reps
2 × 22 yards, 1 forwards and 1 backwards.

Intensity
40 per cent for the first 11 yards and 30 per cent for the second 11 yards.

DRILL CARIOCA

Follow the instructions on page 19.

Aim
To warm down the hips and the core.

Sets and reps
2 × 22 yards, 1 leading with the left leg and one leading with the right.

Intensity
30 per cent for the first 11 yards and 20 per cent for the second 11 yards.

DRILL SMALL SKIP

Follow the instructions on page 11.

Aim
To warm down the muscles of the lower leg and the ankle.

Sets and reps
2 × 22 yards, 1 forwards and 1 backwards.

Intensity
20 per cent for the first 11 yards and 10 per cent for the second 11 yards.

DRILL ANKLE FLICKS

Follow the instructions on page 10.

Aim
To bring the heart rate down and to stretch the calf and ankle.

Sets and reps
2 × 22 yards, 1 forwards and 1 backwards.

Intensity
10 per cent for the first 11 yards and walking for the second 11 yards.

DRILL HURDLE WALK

Follow the instructions on page 24.

Aim
To bring the heart rate down.

Sets and reps
2 × 22 yards, 1 forwards and 1 backwards.

Intensity
Walking.

DRILL WALKING HAMSTRING

Follow the instructions on page 27.

Aim
To stretch the backs of the thighs.

Sets and reps
2 × 22 yards, 1 forwards and 1 backwards.

Intensity
Walking.

DRILL LATISSIMUS DORSI STRETCH

Aim
To stretch the muscles of the back.

Description
Stand in an upright position and link the hands together in front of the chest. Push the hands out, simultaneously arching the back forwards.

Key teaching points
- Do not force the arms out too far
- Focus on slow, controlled breathing

Sets and reps
Hold the stretch for about 10 seconds.

DRILL QUADRICEPS STRETCH

Aim
To stretch and assist the recovery of the thigh muscles.

Description
Stand on one leg and bring the other heel in towards the buttock. Using the hand on that side, hold the instep of the raised foot and squeeze it into the buttock. Repeat on the opposite leg.

Key teaching points
- Keep the knees together
- Ensure the support leg is slightly bent
- Press the hip forwards
- Focus on slow, controlled breathing
- Do not force the stretch, just squeeze gently

Sets and reps
Hold the stretch for about 10 seconds on each leg.

Variation
The exercise can be performed while the player is lying down on their side on the floor

DRILL HAMSTRING STRETCH

Aim
To stretch and assist the recovery of the hamstrings.

Description
Working in pairs, one player raises a leg to a 90-degree angle. The partner holds the back of the heel. The toe of the raised leg is pulled towards the shin (dorsiflexion) and the leg is kept straight as the partner gently raises it.

Key teaching points
- Focus on slow, controlled breathing
- Bend forwards from the hip; do not lean back
- The partner is to assist by raising the leg gently – do not force the stretch

Sets and reps
Hold the stretch for about 10 seconds on each leg.

DRILL ADDUCTORS STRETCH

Aim
To stretch and assist the recovery of the adductor muscles.

Description
Stand with the legs apart, bend one knee and keep the foot at a 45-degree angle. The other leg should be straight. Repeat on the opposite leg.

Key teaching points
- Focus on slow, controlled breathing
- Do not force the stretch
- Keep the back straight
- Do not allow the knee of the bent leg to go beyond the toes

Sets and reps
Hold the stretch for about 10 seconds on each leg.

DRILL CALF STRETCH

Aim
To stretch and assist the recovery of the calf muscles.

Description
Stand with the legs split and both feet pointing forwards, one leg to the front and the other to the back. The weight should be transferred to the forward knee and then gently back. Repeat with the other leg.

Key teaching points
- The front knee should not move further than over the ankle
- The back leg should be kept straight – it is this calf that will be stretched
- Focus on slow, controlled breathing
- Do not force the stretch
- Apply the weight slowly to the front foot

Sets and reps
Hold the stretch for about 10 seconds on each leg.

CHAPTER 11 SAQ TENNIS PROGRAMMES

This chapter provides sample training sessions and programmes for both professional and amateur players. For some players tennis is a summer sport, yet thanks to indoor courts it can be played all year round. For the professional tennis player the game is practically all year round and also includes a great deal of travel.

The key to any programme is how it is periodised throughout the year, plus its ability to recognise individual needs and provide leeway for unscheduled changes. The best programmes are those that are varied, provide challenges, keep the players on their toes and accept individuality. Too much of the same demotivates individuals, therefore performance, including skill and concentration, can be compromised.

Here are some simple rules:

- Start with Dynamic Flex
- Explosive work and sprints should be completed early in the session before any anaerobic work
- Plan sessions so that an 'explosion' session is followed by a preparation day
- Progress from simple drills to complex drills
- Don't restrict programmes to one-week periods; work with different blocks of 4–8–10–12 days
- Teach one new skill a day
- Rest and recovery periods should be well planned
- Vary work-to-rest ratios
- Build up strength before performing plyometrics
- Keep sessions short and sharp: explanations and discussions should be conducted before and afterwards, not in activity time
- Finish off sessions with static (PNF) stretching
- Introduce ice baths, cold showers and recovery sessions after training
- Perform Dynamic Flex drills in the swimming pool as part of an active recovery session

FIVE–WEEK PRE–SEASON PROGRAMME

W E E K 1

MONDAY	Tennis-specific complex weights programme	
TUESDAY	Dynamic Flex warm-up	10 min
	Mechanics	15 min
	Innervation	10 min
	Accumulation	10 min
	Expression	5 min
	Technical tennis drills	25 min
	Tennis interval runs	15 min
	Dynamic Flex warm-down	5 min
WEDNESDAY	Rest and recovery	
	Swimming	
THURSDAY	Dynamic Flex warm-up	10 min
	Mechanics	15 min
	Innervation	10 min
	Accumulation	10 min
	Vision and reaction drills	10 min
	Technical tennis drills	25 min
	Tennis interval runs	15 min
	Dynamic Flex warm-down	5 min
FRIDAY	Tennis-specific complex weights programme	
	Balance, co-ordination, feel and judgement drills	
SATURDAY	Tennis clock endurance runs	
	Jelly ball workout	
SUNDAY	Rest and recovery	
	Swimming	

WEEK 2

MONDAY	Tennis-specific complex weights programme	
TUESDAY	Dynamic Flex warm-up	10 min
	Mechanics	12 min
	Innervation	12 min
	Accumulation	8 min
	Explosion	10 min
	Expression	5 min
	Technical tennis drills	25 min
	Tennis interval runs	15 min
	Dynamic Flex warm-down	5 min
WEDNESDAY	Rest and recovery	
	Swimming	
THURSDAY	Dynamic Flex warm-up	10 min
	Mechanics	10 min
	Innervation	10 min
	Accumulation	5 min
	Explosion	15 min
	Vision and reaction drills	10 min
	Technical tennis drills	25 min
	Tennis interval runs	15 min
	Dynamic Flex warm-down	5 min
FRIDAY	Tennis-specific complex weights programme	
	Balance, co-ordination, feel and judgement drills	
SATURDAY	Tennis clock endurance runs	
	Jelly ball workout	
SUNDAY	Rest and recovery	
	Swimming	

W E E K   3

MONDAY	Tennis-specific complex weights programme	
TUESDAY	Dynamic Flex warm-up	10 min
	Mechanics	6 min
	Innervation	8 min
	Accumulation	5 min
	Explosion	20 min
	Expression	5 min
	Technical tennis drills	25 min
	Tennis interval runs	15 min
	Dynamic Flex warm-down	5 min
WEDNESDAY	Rest and recovery	
	Swimming	
THURSDAY	Dynamic Flex warm-up	10 min
	Mechanics	5 min
	Innervation	5 min
	Accumulation	10 min
	Explosion	20 min
	Vision and reaction drills	10 min
	Technical tennis drills	25 min
	Tennis interval runs	15 min
	Dynamic Flex warm-down	5 min
FRIDAY	Tennis-specific complex weights programme	
	Balance, co-ordination, feel and judgement drills	
SATURDAY	Tennis clock endurance runs	
	Jelly ball workout	
SUNDAY	Rest and recovery	
	Swimming	

WEEK 4

MONDAY	Tennis-specific complex weights programme	
TUESDAY	Dynamic Flex warm-up	10 min
	Mechanics	5 min
	Innervation	5 min
	Accumulation	10 min
	Explosion	25 min
	Expression	5 min
	Technical tennis drills	25 min
	Tennis interval runs	15 min
	Dynamic Flex warm-down	5 min
WEDNESDAY	Rest and recovery	
	Swimming	
THURSDAY	Dynamic Flex warm-up	10 min
	Accumulation	15 min
	Explosion	25 min
	Vision and reaction drills	10 min
	Technical tennis drills	25 min
	Tennis interval runs	15 min
	Dynamic Flex warm-down	5 min
FRIDAY	Tennis-specific complex weights programme	
	Balance, co-ordination, feel and judgement drills	
SATURDAY	Tennis clock endurance runs	
	Jelly ball workout	
SUNDAY	Rest and recovery	
	Swimming	

W E E K   5

MONDAY	Tennis-specific complex weights programme	
TUESDAY	Dynamic Flex warm-up	10 min
	Accumulation	15 min
	Explosion	25 min
	Expression	5 min
	Technical tennis drills	25 min
	Tennis interval runs	15 min
	Dynamic Flex warm-down	5 min
WEDNESDAY	Rest and recovery	
	Swimming	
THURSDAY	Dynamic Flex warm-up	10 min
	Accumulation	10 min
	Explosion	30 min
	Vision and reaction drills	10 min
	Technical tennis drills	25 min
	Tennis interval runs	15 min
	Dynamic Flex warm-down	5 min
FRIDAY	Tennis-specific complex weights programme	
	Balance, co-ordination, feel and judgement drills	
SATURDAY	Tennis clock endurance runs	
	Jelly ball workout	
SUNDAY	Rest and recovery	
	Swimming	

WEEKLY AMATEUR IN-SEASON PROGRAMME FOR WEEKEND TENNIS PLAYERS

MONDAY	Dynamic Flex warm-up	12 min
	Mechanics	
	Arm mechanics mirror drills	3 sets of 16 reps, 1-minute recovery between reps
	Dead-leg run	3 sets of 8 reps, 4 leading with left leg, 4 leading with right, 1-minute recovery between each set
	Pre-turn	
	Lateral shuffle step	3 sets of 8 reps, 4 leading with left leg, 4 leading with right, 1-minute recovery between each set
	Innervation	
	Single run	3 sets of 6 reps, 1-minute recovery between each set
	Single lateral steps	3 sets of 6 reps, 1-minute recovery between each set
	Icky shuffle	3 sets of 6 reps, 1-minute recovery between each set
	Explosion	
	Seated forward get-up	3 sets of 5 reps, 2-minute recovery between each set
	Flexi-cord out and back	3 sets of 6 reps plus 1 contrast run, 3-minute recovery between each set
	Vision and reaction	
	Reaction ball work	2 sets of 20 reps, 1-minute recovery between each set
	Dynamic Flex warm-down	
TUESDAY	Dynamic Flex warm-up	12 min
	Tennis-specific endurance runs	
	Dynamic Flex warm-down	
WEDNESDAY	Rest and recovery	
	Swimming	
THURSDAY	Dynamic Flex warm-up	12 min

(Contd)...

WEEKLY AMATEUR IN–SEASON PROGRAMME FOR WEEKEND TENNIS PLAYERS *(Contd)...*

Day	Activity	**Mechanics**
	Buttock bounce	3 sets of 8 reps, 1-minute recovery between each set
	Leading leg run	3 sets of 8 reps, 4 leading with left leg, 4 leading with right, 1-minute recovery between each set
	Quick side-step development	2 sets of 10 reps, 5 leading with left leg, 5 leading with right, 1-minute recovery between each set
	Lateral step/shuffle development	2 sets of 3 reps with a walk-back recovery between reps, 2-minute recovery between each set
	Innervation	
	Double run	3 sets of 6 reps, 1-minute recovery between each set
	Single-space jumps	3 sets of 6 reps, 1-minute recovery between each set
	2 forwards, 1 back	3 sets of 6 reps, 1-minute recovery between each set
	Hopscotch	3 sets of 6 reps, 1-minute recovery between each set
	Explosion	
	Flexi-cord resistance W drill	3 sets of 5 reps, 2-minute recovery between each set
	Handweight drops	3 sets of 4 reps, 3-minute recovery between each set
	Vision and reaction	
	Fast hands	30 seconds each drill × 5, 10-second recovery between each set
	Balance, co-ordination, feel and judgement	
	Feel and distance drill	Empty the basket of balls
	Dynamic Flex warm-down	
FRIDAY	Dynamic Flex warm-up	12 min
	Tennis clock endurance runs	4 sets with 2-minute recovery between each set
SATURDAY AND SUNDAY	Match days	■ Always perform Dynamic Flex before playing ■ Always perform Dynamic Flex warm-down after playing ■ Ensure you maintain a high level of hydration, even in cold weather ■ Cold showers after playing aid recovery

Glossary

Acceleration   Increasing velocity, specifically over the first 25 yards.

Aerobic   Energy system that uses oxygen.

Agility   The ability to move quickly in any direction and maintain balance.

Anaerobic   Energy system that does not rely on oxygen to function.

ATP   Adenosine Triphosphate – the only source of energy that muscle can utilise. All food gets broken down into this molecule.

Competitive skills   Skills such as running, jumping or lateral movement that can be used in the sporting environment.

Contrast   A stage after that of resistance where the player/athlete performs the same drill but is unresisted.

Dorsiflexion   Flexing the ankle by lifting the toes, as if one were trying to lift up a bucket with one's toe.

Dynamic   Any movements, particularly those involving stretches, that actively move a limb through its full range of motion.

Explosive   The ability to generate great amounts of force in a very short space of time.

Fast-twitch fibres   Present in larger proportions in explosive/power athletes, enabling them to perform explosive, powerful movements, as opposed to endurance athletes, who possess a greater number of slow-twitch fibres.

Flexibility   Range of motion about a joint. Also the ability of a joint to be elongated.

Force application   Ability to generate the summation of synchronised force to be applied at a specific point in time or space, e.g. when throwing a ball.

Goals   An important part of mental preparation in which one thinks about and decides what one wants to achieve.

Hops   Single-leg repeated movements

Jumps   Double-leg repeated movements

Lactate   Leftover by-product of anaerobic metabolism that is converted back into ATP by the liver.

Maximum speed   Fastest speed obtainable by an individual, usually achieved between 30 and 50 yards.

Muscular efficiency   The use of stores of muscle energy in a manner that is not wasteful to the athlete, through minimising and

	eliminating wasted movements.
Neuromuscular recruitment	Activities that work to activate more muscle units.
Peripheral vision	Ability to see things or movements while focusing on another object.
Plantar flexion	Pointing the toes downwards from the ankle, i.e. full extension of the ankle.
Plyometrics	Any activity that utilises the stretch reflex, eliciting rapid changes between eccentric and concentric contractions.
PNF	Proprioreceptive Neuromuscular Facilitation – a form of training that improves flexibility by increasing the strength of the agonist/primary muscle while decreasing the resistance of the antagonist.

Power output	The rate at which work is done.
Progressive overload	In training, the concept that one needs constantly to force the body to adapt to new stresses.
Proprioception	One's ability to adjust to any stimulus. Can be applied directly to or around the body.
Quicker	To generate a movement in a shorter space of time.
Resistance	A type of training that involves tools to increase the force required to move.
Specificity	Training precisely for the demands of your sport or skill development.
Speed	The ability to move fast over a specific distance.
Strength	The raw ability to overcome gravitational or applied forces.

References

Bennett, S. (1999), 'New Muscle Research Findings', *Muscle Symposium*, AIS, Canberra, Australia

Ferrauti, A. and Weber, K. (2001), *Stroke situations in clay court tennis*, Unpublished data

Gallahue, D. L. and Cleland Donnelly, F. (2003), *Developmental Physical Education for All Youngsters*, Human Kinetics, New York

Gleim, G. W. and McHugh, M. P. (1997), 'Flexibility and Its Effects on Sports Injury and Performance', *Sports Medicine*, 24(5): 289–99

Haake, S. J. and Coe, A. O. (2000), *Tennis Science and Technology*, International Tennis Federation

Hennessy, L. Dr (2000), 'Developing Explosive Power', Paper, SAQ Symposium, June 2000

Herbert, R. D. and Gabriel, M. (2002), 'Effects of stretching before or after exercising on muscle soreness and risk of injury: a systematic review', *The British Medical Journal*, 325: 468–70.

Kokkonen, J., Nelson A. G. and Cornwell, A. (1998), 'Acute muscle stretching inhibits maximal strength performance', *Research Quarterly for Exercise and Sport*, Vol. 4, pp. 411–15, 1998

McMillian, D. J., Moore, J. H., Hatler, B. S. and Taylor, D.C. (2005), *Heidelberg Medical Activity, Apo, AE, USA* 'Dynamic Versus Static Stretching Warm-Up: The Effect on Power and Agility Performance', *The British Medical Journal*, Vol. 39 p. 396

Oberg, B. (1993), 'Evaluation and improvement of strength in competitive athletes', in Harms-Ringdahl, K. (ed.) *Muscle Strength* (pp 167–85), Churchill Livingstone, Edinburgh.

Nike Sports Research Lab (2004), Research summary: Nike Free booklet

Pope, R. C. (1999), 'Skip the Warm-up', *New Scientist*, 18 Dec 164(2214):23

Reid, M., Quinn, A. and Crespo, M. (2003), *Strength and Conditioning for Tennis*, International Tennis Federation

Roetert, E. P. and Ellenbecker, T. S. (1998), *Complete Conditioning for Tennis*, Human Kinetics, Champaign, Illinois

Roetert, E. P., Ellenbecker, T. S. and Chu, D. (2003), *Strength and Conditioning for Tennis*, International Tennis Federation

Rosenbaum, D. and Hennig, E. M. (1995), 'The influence of stretching and warm-up exercises on Achilles tendon reflex activity', Journal of Sports Sciences, 13: 481–90

Smith, L. L., Brunetz, M. H., Cheiner, T. C., McCammon, M. R., Houmard, J. A., Franklin, M. E. and Israel, R. G. (1993), 'The effects of static and ballistic stretching on DOMS and Creatin Kinase', Research Quarterly for Exercise and Sport, 64(1)L, 103–7

Smythe, R. (2000). 'Acts of Agility', *Training and conditioning*, 5(4): 22–5

Sugden, D. A., Talbot, M., Utley, A., Vickerman, P., Thomas, N. and Cook, B. (1998) 'Physical Education for children with special educational needs', Sports Council Vol. 2

Walkley, J., Holland, B., Treolar, R. and Probyn-Smith, H. (1993), 'Fundamental motor skill proficiency of children', *ACHPER National Journal*, 40(3), 11–14

Index of drills